The Anglo-Russian Entente Cordiale

of 1697-1698

Peter I and William III at Utrecht

GEORGE BARANY

EAST EUROPEAN MONOGRAPHS, BOULDER
DISTRIBUTED BY COLUMBIA UNIVERSITY PRESS, NEW YORK

1986

EAST EUROPEAN MONOGRAPHS, NO. CCVII

Copyright © 1986 by George Barany
Library of Congress Card Catalog Number 86-80412
ISBN 0-88033-104-6

Printed in the United States of America

To Ernestine, my wife

CONTENTS

LIST OF ILLUSTRATIONS

ACKNOWLEDGMENT

Chance, that unpredictable contributor to history, often tricks its student. While doing research in the Sutherland Papers recently deposited in the National Library of Scotland at Edinburgh, my eye was caught by a handwritten document which I thought might be of interest to students of Russian history. This happened in the autumn of 1982; identification and analysis of the document and efforts to place it into the proper historical context took much of my time in subsequent years before drafts of the present *opusculum* could be submitted to friends for critical scrutiny. In the process of probing into the personal relationships of two giants of world history and the political environment that surrounded them, I learned a lot.

In the initial phase of my research I had the benefit of a grant from the American Philosophical Society, Philadelphia, which enabled me to work in English and Scottish archives and libraries. I followed up my preliminary findings, thanks to the assistance of the International Research and Exchange Board and the Fulbright-Hays Faculty Abroad Program of the United States Department of Education, during my sabbatical in 1984-1985, part of which I spent in Hungary, Austria and the United Kingdom.

In the course of my work I was greatly helped by the friendly advice of librarians and archivists in half a dozen countries, including those at my own institution, especially in the Interlibrary Loan Service and Rare Book Collection. Their help is gratefully registered in the notes appended to this study.

I am in the debt of a number of colleagues and distinguished teacher-editor friends, such as Professors John C. Livingston at the University of Denver; Max J. Okenfuss, Washington University, St. Louis, Missouri; Nicholas V. Riasanovsky, University of California, Berkeley; Boyd C. Shafer, University of Arizona, Tucson; and Donald W. Treadgold, University of Washington, Seattle, for their helpful criticism of earlier versions of the present study. The professional guidance of the editor of the East European Monograph Series, Professor Stephen Fischer-Galati, is also deeply appreciated, as is the artistic talent of the graphics designer, Anne D'E. Fisher.

My special thanks are due to the Countess of Sutherland for her gracious hospitality and kind permission to do research in the family archives. Although my original inquiry was related to a different subject, I should like to hope that the redirection of my interest, resulting from the discovery of the manuscript of the "Czar of Muscovys Speech when he met King William at Utrecht" will not have been entirely in vain.

A final word of gratitude to my wife, Ernestine, for her meticulous reading and patient critique of a text abounding in pitfalls.

I

Introduction

In an article published over a quarter of a centry ago,[1] Leo
Loewenson noted the significance of the first personal meeting
on September 1/11, 1697, between William III of England and
Peter I, the tsar of Muscovy, future Emperor of All the Russias.
Surveying the Russian, French, Dutch, German and English
historical literature, he pointed out that although the date of
the two rulers' meeting at Utrecht and the official circumstances surrounding it had been sufficiently clarified, "our
knowledge of essential details is far from being satisfactory."[2]
In view of the silence of Russian sources regarding the "private"
interview and the criticism raised concerning some of the information contained in non-Russian accounts, Loewenson cited
excerpts from previously neglected manuscripts and contemporary printed sources in England to shed new light on the first
encounter between tsar and king.

   Crucial to Loewenson's study was his interpretation of a
speech Peter allegedly made when he first met William. Two
French versions of this speech had appeared in print in 1721
and 1742 and they were later reprinted in an appendix of a Russian work on the two hundredth anniversary of the "Great

1

Embassy"'s visit to Holland, but early nineteenth century
Dutch authors had doubted its authenticity.[3] Later Russian and
Soviet historians even suggested that the address attributed to the
tsar "appears to be the fruit of the phantasy of his foreign bio-
graphers."[4] Yet Loewenson argued that "Peter's speech" did
not constitute a "posthumous invention of some 18th-century
writer," that several copies of it had been in circulation in late
1697, and that it was based on the tsar's actual utterances. He
also claimed that the speech and the gestures of friendship with
which the king responded to it mirrored the informality and
cordial atmosphere which prevailed at the early meetings of
Peter and William.[5] Further, Loewenson believed that the first
French version of the speech printed in London in 1697 and
republished by him *in toto* was the original which served as a
basis for later English and even Dutch abstracts.[6] It is noteworthy that a copy of this French sheet, preserved in the British
Museum, was apparently placed at Voltaire's disposal for his
History of the Russian Empire under Peter the Great; although
deposited in St. Petersburg after having been acquired by
Catherine the Great, this French version of Peter's Utrecht
address was ignored by both Russian historiography,[7] and
Voltaire himself.

Loweenson's imaginative study did not receive the attention
it deserves.[8] To be sure, the author knew that the material available to him did not allow a definitive determination of the
precise relationship of the different versions of the speech and
that "a final solution of the problem" was impossible "without
a complete knowledge of all the circumstances connected with
the Utrecht interview."[9] Nevertheless, his research contributes
greatly to our understanding of the encounter which took place
during the last phase of the peace negotiations on the eve of the
signing of the Treaty of Ryswick in which Louis XIV agreed to
recognize the Prince of Orange and Stadholder of Holland as
King of England, ending a nine-year-long general European
war.[10]

The recent identification of an English version of the tsar's speech, unknown to Loewenson, corroborates most of his findings and even allows us a fuller understanding of the two monarchs' first meetings on Dutch soil. After a critical scrutiny of the newly found text, this study will examine the broader military-political and economic background of the Utrecht encounter, turning subsequently to its implications in Central Europe and indeed in the global alliance systems existing in the *clair-obscur* of the transition from one general European conflagration to two major military conflicts, fought for the Spanish succession and for supremacy in Northern and Eastern Europe, respectively.

The Czar of Muscovys Speech to King William
when he mett him at Utrecht

Most Renowned Empire

It was not the desire of seeing the Celebrated Cities
of the German Empire; or the most Potent Republick of
the Universe, that made me leave my Throne in a Distant
Country, and my Victorious Armies. but the Vehement
Passion alone of seeing the most Brave and most Generous
Hero of the age

I have my wish; and am Sufficiently recompinced
for my Travell in being admitted into Your Presence; Your
Kind Embraces have given me more Sattisfaction than the
takeing of Azoph and Triumphking over the Tartars. But the
Conquest is Yours, Your Martiall Genious directed my Sword
And the Generous Emulation of your Exploits Instilled into
my Breast the first thoughto I had of Enlarging my Dominions

I Cannot express in words the Veneration I have for
Your Sacred Person my Unparaleld Journey is one Proof of it

The Season is so far advanced, and I hope the peace
Too that I shall not have the Opertunitey as Maximillian
had of Fighting under the Banner of England against
France the Common &c

If the War continues I and my Armies will
readly Observe Your Orders and if either in War or Peace
Your Industrious Subjects will Trade to the most Northern
parts of the world the ports of Russia shall be free for
them I will grant them greater Immunities than ever they
Yet had and have them Enrolld among the most precious
Records of My Empire to be a perpetual Memorial of
the Esteem I have for the Worthiest of Kings

II

Summit at Utrecht: Under the Banner of England

A document found among the Sutherland Papers, in the Department of Manuscripts of the National Library of Scotland in Edinburgh, may help clarify some of the ambiguities surrounding Peter's first meeting with William.[11] Handwritten and undated, it purports to be "The Czar of Muscovys Speech to King William when he mett him at Utrecht." (*Sic*) Following the original orthography and arrangement of the lines and words, the text of the document reads:[12]

> The Czar of Muscoyys Speech to King William
> when he mett him at Utrecht

Most Renowned Emper

> It was not the desire of seeing the Celebrated Cities
> of the German Empire; or the most Potent Repúblick of
> the Uuniverse, that made me leave My Throne in a Distant
> Coúntry, And my Victorious Armies but the Vehement
> Passion alone of seeing the most Brave and most Generous
> Hero of the Age
> I have my wish; and am Sufficiently recompenced
> for my Travell in being admited into Your Presence; Your
> Kind Embraces have given me more Sattisfaction than the

takeing of Azoph and Triumphing over the Tartars, But the
Conquest is Yours, Your Martial Genioús directed my sword
And the Generous Emulation of your Exploits Instilled into
my Breast the first thoughts I had of Enlarging my Dominions
   I Cannot express in words the veneration I have for
Your Sacred Person my Unparaleld Journey is one Proof of it
   The Season is so farr advaced, that I hope the Peace
Too that I shall not have the Opertuinety as Maximillian
had of Fighting under the Banner of England against
France the Common etc.

   If the Warr continúes I and my Armies will
readly Observe Your Orders and if either in Warr or Peace
Your Indústruoús Subjects will Trade to the most Northern
Parts of the world the Ports of Russia shall be free for
them I will grant them greater Immúnities than ever they
Yet had and have them Enroll'd among the most Precious
Records of My Empire to be a perpetual Memorial of
the Esteem I have for the Worthiest of Kings.

   The inconsistencies of orthography, punctuation and the use
of capitals characteristic of Elizabethan handwriting, some of
which survived into the late eighteenth century, are reflected in
the original of the transcript reproduced above. Although rapid
progress toward the standardization of English spelling began in
the latter half of the seventeenth century,[13] the manuscript of
Peter's speech could not have been written before his visit to
Utrecht in 1697. The abbreviations in the opening salutation addressed to William III and at the end of the penultimate paragraph suggest that the English text was not intended for publi-
cation.

   Further textual ctiticism and a comparison of the different
variants of the tsar's speech will also show that

a) the handwritten copy in the National Library of Scotland
   is the most direct and complete of all English texts known
   to us hitherto;
b) that it is almost identical with the French version of 1697;
   and

c) that if not the original text of Peter's address, it may be the variant closest to it on which other abstracts and translations, including the earliest deposited in the British Museum, are based.

If our hypothesis proves to be true, some of the assumptions and conclusions of Loewenson's article may have to be reconsidered without necessarily questioning its main thesis, namely, that Peter's speech was indeed delivered and warrants further historical analysis.

III

"A Mighty Northern Emperour"

Of the three contemporary English documents revealing awareness of Peter's speech, the abstract in Narcissus Luttrell's day-by-day chronicle of contemporary events covering the period 1678-1714 is the most detailed. Quoted frequently as an authoritative source by Lord Macauley in his *History of England,* Luttrell's chronicle includes "the czars speech to his majestie" under the date of October 14, 1697. Loewenson had regarded this summary a "direct version" and "purified form" of the French text printed in 1697, the style and verbiage of which was alien to Peter in his opinion.[14] But a comparison of Luttrell's sober abstract with the Edinburgh version of the tsar's address shows that the former is an abridgment of the English text transcribed above rather than a condensed translation of the contemporary French variant. Other than the use of the third person and the repeated reference to "his majestie", the summary incorporates some of the orthographic characters (travell) and expressions of the complete English rather than the French text. ("To see the most brave" and "kind embraces" instead of "Visiter le plus Brave" and "doux Accueil".) In those few instances when the Edinburgh manuscript and the British Museum's

8

printed French deviate from each other, Luttrell's short abstract follows the former. ("He and his armies were at his majesties service" instead of "Je manderai aux Generaux de mes Armées de se tenir prêts à suivre incessamment Vos Ordres" and "His ports should be free to his majesties subjects" instead of "les Ports de la Russie leur seront libres & ouverts.") Given the brevity of the abstract, these and other linguistic examples ("greater immunities then (*sic*) they ever yet have had") strongly suggest that the compiler of the summary had an English rather than French text before him.

Similarly revealing is the term "extending the limits of his Dominions" in another abstract of the speech quoted by Loewenson from a mid-eighteenth century English *Metalick History* which explained the reason for the commemorative medal struck on the occasion of the Utrecht encounter of William and Peter.[15] The French text of 1697 mentions "d'aggrandir mon Empire" as does that of 1721; interestingly, however, the 1742 French edition speaks of "d'agrandir mes Etats" which, along with other examples to be enumerated below, suggests that its author was familiar with the full text of the English version of the speech and considered it more authentic than its French counterpart.

A passage in the sermon given at Whitehall in the presence of king and court by Bishop Burnet on December 2, 1697, is also noteworthy. The occasion was the Thanksgiving service held after William's return to England from the Ryswick peace negotiations in mid-November. In the sermon, the distinguished theologian-historian lauded the king as the divinely inspired architect of victory who had brought peace to England and Europe as well. After drawing a parallel between William and the biblical king Solomon, he turned to the chosen scriptural text for the day, which dealt with the visit of the queen of Sheba to Jerusalem, attracted by Solomon's wisdom:

And to make the Parallel to my Text run exactly, a much greater King, lying at a vaster Distance, leaves his Throne and Dominions in the midst of War, stuck with the Fame and Amazed at the Actions of this Prince. Instead of a little Southern Queen, a mighty Northern Emperour, cover'd with Laurels, and us'd to Victories, resolving to raise his Nation, and enlarge his Empire, comes to learn the best Methods of doing it, and goes away full of Wonder, possessed with truer Notions of Government.[16]

The ideas and images echoing the first two paragraphs of Peter's Utrecht speech, combined with the allusions to the tsar and his admiration of William expressed in the paragraph just quoted supports Loewenson's observation that the text of the speech had been in circulation within a few weeks after the two rulers' encounter; obviously, Burnet must have been familiar with it.[17] This was no mere coincidence. As pointed out by James Cracraft, who stressed the importance of the tsar's repeated and often very long personal meetings with the bishop of Salisbury during his three-month stay in England, the king himself ordered Burnet to attend upon Peter. But many months before they met in person, the bishop received reliable information about the tsar from the German philosopher-scientist Gottfried Wilhelm Leibniz.[18] As evidenced by the Thanksgiving sermon, Burnet's expectations were further stimulated by Peter's speech made at Utrecht and, possibly, by the personal account he may have received about the meeting from the king or one of his confidants.

All this, however, does not mean that the passage cited from the Thanksgiving sermon was based on the French version, as Loewenson assumed. The most prominent churchman of the Age of the Glorious Revolution returned to England from the Netherlands with William and Mary in 1688; he knew both Dutch and French.[19] Theoretically, Burnet could have used either a French or an English, or even a Dutch text of the speech. The freely flowing pertinent sentences in his Thanksgiving sermon convey the tenor of the speech and the hopes attached to it by the bishop rather than direct quotations. Although the term "enlarge his Empire" insinuates awareness of the French text, the expression "leaves his Throne and Dominions" arouses suspicion because, as indicated above, the word "Dominions" occurs only in the full English Edinburgh variant. Even more decisive is the reference to "a much greater King, lying at a vaster Distance." This phrase corresponds to "a Distant Country" left by the tsar according to the English text. But the French edition of 1697 insinuates that it was Peter who came to a distant land ("pour venir dans un Pays éloigné;"). This reversal of the tsar's perspective is absent from Burnet's interpretation which is thus directly related to the Edinburgh copy and not its French counterpart. One may note that this particular formulation of the French version of 1697 is missing from both the 1721 and 1742 published French variants.

If one carefully collates the French and English texts of 1697, one cannot help being struck by the near-identity of the two. Leaving aside the fancier title of the French and the last sentence indicating where the printed sheet can be bought (which is missing from the English), the opening salutation of the address and the five short paragraphs in it are identical. Indeed at first glance the two texts are deceptively similar, as indicated by the unfinished last sentence of the penultimate paragraph which ends on "etc." in both the English and French versions ("contre la France, le Commun, etc."). While the French 1721 edition explains and supplements what was common knowledge in 1697 by referring to "la France, la commune ennemie de la chretienté",[20] the translator-editor of 1742, who may have found the phrase anachronistic or politically inopportune, omitted it entirely. The discrepancies, some of which have been mentioned previously, are not many, but they are worth examining.

The first of these appears in the title of the printed French, which is more formal and indirect than that of the English

("Compliment du Grand CZAR de Muscovie, au ROI de la
Grand' Bretagne, a Utrecht.") Of the remaining eight differ-
ences in the formulation of essentially analogous ideas, six were
touched upon in connection with the abstract of the speech in
Luttrell's *Diary,* the texts pertinent to the commemorative
medal and to Burnet's Thanksgiving sermon. The other two
minor discrepancies are stylistic.

As indicated earlier, whenever an abridged text or fragment of
the speech was paraphrased in English, the Edinburgh version
prevailed over the French edition of 1697. With the sole exception of the divergence involving the problem of the speaker's
perspective, omitted from both eighteenth century French editions of the speech, the French text of 1742 follows, in every
instance where there is a discrepancy, i.e., seven times, the English
of the Edinburgh copy in translation rather than the presumed
original French of 1697 ("célèbres villes," "voir le plus brave
héros," "tendres embrassements," "je Vous suis redevable de la
Conquête," "d'agrandir mes Etats," "je suis prêt à suivre Vos
ordres," "tous les ports leur y seront ouverts"). This remarkable sequence prompts us to revise Loewenson's contention that
"each successive edition of the French text contains a fresh
sprinkling of rhetoric and that, owing in particular to omissions,
the wording of the latest version (1742) deviated from the earliest French text (1697) quite considerably." While it is true that
several passages of the 1721 French edition follow the 1697
French version very closely,[21] the shorter 1742 text constitutes
an independent translation whose author may have been familiar
with earlier French texts too and did not refrain from "editing"
them but essentially relied on an English text which he regarded
as the original.

Another fascinating aspect to the "mystery" surrounding
Peter's speech is the question of why Voltaire, who as Loewenson said, had the 1697 French printed sheet, failed to mention
it. Immensely knowledgeable about the age of Louis XIV,
Charles XII and Peter I, he wrote meticulous histories of all three

personalities; at the time of writing his learned *Histoire de l'-Empire de Russie sous Pierre le Grand* (1759-1762), Voltaire was aware of "several pretended histories of Peter the Great" which, along with other works on political and military leaders, he regarded as "printed frauds altogether too common." In his "Historical and Critical Preface" to the history of Peter's Russia, the "Sage of Ferney" stressed that "Never did history stand more in need of authentic proofs than in our days, when there is such insolent traffic in lies."[22] Is it perhaps because of this noble principle that Voltaire elected to ignore not only the 1697 French version of Peter's speech but also the later editions of which he must have been aware?[23]

The question is the more intriguing because Voltaire specifically does mention the tsar's meeting, "without ceremony," with William at Utrecht and the Hague. Relying on the Englishman John Perry, who had been in the service of Peter, and whose book on *The State of Russia Under the Present Czar* was first printed in 1716, and General Franz Lefort, the official head of the Great Embassy whose manuscripts were placed at his disposal by the Court of St. Petersburg, Voltaire emphasizes the private nature of these encounters, adding that Lefort was the only other person present.[24] Although Lefort's mid-nineteenth century biography conveys the same view, Loewenson, referring to Luttrell's *Diary* and contemporary English newspaper reports, claims that it is far from certain how many people attended the first and possibly a secnd meeting of king and tsar at Utrecht, and who acted as interpreter.[25] But even if Lefort was the interpreter, this does not necessarily prove that French was the language used in the informal exchanges between William and Peter. The Geneva-born Lefort had been in the Dutch service before he moved to Muscovy and the tsar also knew Dutch well before his arrival in Holland; in fact, he would avail himself of that language in Brandenburg on occasion when communicating with members of his retinue and unwilling to have his Prussian hosts understand him. We also know from Peter's first interview with Leopold I when Lefort translated the tsar's Russian words into German, a language in which Peter was much weaker than in Dutch, that he would occasionally interrupt his interpreter, asking him to explain a point more fully to the emperor.[26]

All this implies that the Russian historian Venevitinov's doubt regarding the genuineness of two eighteenth-century French versions of Peter's speech, namely, that these translations "were made from some sort of identical source, probably written initially in Dutch or English"[27] may also apply to the 1697 French edition. Indeed, as shown by its title, the latter may be a somewhat embellished but on the whole faithful and complete translation of the English manuscript preserved in the Sutherland Papers. Yet even if correct, this assumption does not necessarily prove that the Edinburgh manuscript is the original of Peter's speech. Written in an unhurried calligraphy, the manuscript is probably a transcript of a text or notes jotted down by someone present at the meeting, perhaps a translator or scribe, as Sir John Barrow suspected.[28]

While the existence of a slightly simpler but still sufficiently flowery, and apparently complete, English version of Peter's speech tends to refute Loewenson's belief that the original was conceived in French, it affirms his argument that such an address was indeed given, possibly in the form of an improvised toast, at the time of the first meeting at Utrecht, as intimated by the wording of the title of the Edinburgh copy. The co-existence of the near-identical early French variant and its likely English source does not totally eliminate the possibility of a contemporary fake which is also alluded by Loewenson. But this imposes on us an added obligation to investigate in depth that "essence of the text" which Loewenson thought as "in keeping with Peter's mind and mood at the time," especially "such historically correct features as Peter's attitude to William III, or his anti-French bias."[29]

IV

Double Election in Poland: the Challenge of France

A fuller historical analysis of the tsar's address seems justified because a critical textual examination alone does not answer the question, why did Voltaire choose to remain silent on the subject. As stated above, the English manuscript at Edinburgh seems to be very close to the original and reveals sentiments and ideas expressed by the tsar, perhaps in Dutch when he met King William. Loewenson's article has furnished convincing evidence that there were several English copies circulating among the king's confidants. Yet aside from fragments or abstracts, the text of the address was never published in English, while its French version found its way into print in London even before Peter set foot on British soil. Was this a case of anti-French propaganda in which some court circles might have had a hand, perhaps even to the point of fabricating the speech itself? While such a hypothesis could explain Voltaire's attitude, it is contradicted by the circumstance that highranking supporters of William who were in a position to know, such as Bishop Burnet or the first owner of the Edinburgh copy obviously believed in the authenticity of the address. But if the speech, or its "essence" as Loewenson called it, was genuine, did it mean anything beyond the

tsar's youthful enthusiasm about William for whom, in the
words of a modern writer, "he had conceived a certain hero-
worship"?[30] If so, what was the stadholder-king's reaction to
such an outpouring of affection? In order to come to grips with
these questions, a look at the circumstances that surrounded
the meeting at Utrecht is indicated.

In his monograph on the Russians in Holland, Venevitinov
elaborated on the encounter at Utrecht. Relying on Russian
diplomatic reports, he stressed the private and unofficial character of the meeting. At the same time, he described in detail
the number of coaches, horses and riders in William's retinue,
the honor guard, and the applauding throng gathered in front
of the house where the Russian delegation was lodged, as well
as the protocol observed by the Russian ambassadors in greeting their royal guest in the special room reserved from them before the "talks took place." But, as Venevitinov noted, Russian
sources not only remained silent regarding the thrust of these
talks, but also failed to mention Peter by name.[31]

The silence of contemporary Russian documents on Peter,
let alone his active participation in the exchanges at Utrecht
is not surprising in view of the strict instructions of the Russian
Embassy to ignore the tsar's presence but otherwise observe the
regimented protocol of the times.[32] As to the meeting itself,
Peter's Soviet biographer, Bogoslovskii also asserts that "what
the subject of the conversation at this encounter was remains
unknown." Yet, quoting a report by the envoy of the newly
elected king of Poland, Augustus, Bogoslovskii adds that in his
talks with William, Peter touched, "among others," on Polish
affairs and promised to assist with troops the newly elected
Polish King Augustus II. Moreover, he published in full the effusive Latin ode about Peter's conference with William praising
the cooperation of the two most powerful empires of Europe
and Asia. Included too was another poem, extolling the merits
of Nicholas Witsen, Burgomaster of Amsterdam, and an old
friend of Muscovy's who also attended the meeting, rejoiced in

the "embrace of the two caesars," "our liberation from French violence" by William and "Mohammed's defeat by Peter's sword."[33] If one also recalls the commemorative medal struck on the occasion, one is led to the conclusion that given the "private" nature of the interview, it received impressive publicity in the contemporary media, at least in Great Britain and Holland.

Turning to the text of the tsar's address, one cannot help noticing that there were rather modest references to the Russian victories at Azov and over the Tatars in the first two paragraphs, followed by the allusion to the imminence of peace and the still existing alternative of war in the last two. This seeming ambiguity is attributable to the fact that whereas the September 11 meeting between the tsar and the king did actually occur on the eve of the conclusion of the war with Louis XIV, negotiations were still in progress. The French did not sign the peace treaty with England and the United Provinces until September 20, and with the Holy Roman Empire until October 30.[34] Thus Peter's offer to join the anti-French coalition was a real possibility.

The incomplete phrase "Maximillian . . . fighting under the Banner of England against France the Common etc." is of particular interest because it implies that the person recording, perhaps in haste, the speech took it for granted that everybody knew who the common enemy was. While the 1697 French edition agrees verbatim with the English of the Edinburgh copy on this point, the 1721 version belabors the idea by speaking of "the enemy of Christianity" and the "Emperor Maximillian." From the corresponding passage of the 1742 French, which, as we have seen often follows the English rather than the earlier French text, "peace of Europe" rather than peace in general is mentioned, and the name of Maximilian and the references to England and France are absent, the emphasis being only on Peter's desire of "fighting under your banners."

The Maximilian in Peter's speech, known without further identification to both him and William, was Maximilian II

2. Medal struck on the occasion of the retaking of Namur by the joint forces of the King of England and the Elector of Bavaria in 1695. Courtesy Penrose Library, Rare Book Collection, University of Denver, Denver, Colorado. Source: *The Metalic History of the Three Last Reigns*, Plate XVIII, no. 10 and p. 31, appended to vol. IV (1744) of *The History of England*. Written by Mr. [Paul de] Rapin de Thoyras. Translated into English with Additional Notes by N. Tindal. 2d ed. (London, 1732-47).

Front: Hercules clothed with the skin of the Nemean lion stands between a dragon and Cerberus, the three-headed dog holding
the pictures of William III and Maximilian Emanuel. The
legend reads: "Their triumphs prove their deeds."
Reverse: The city of Namur with its fortifications. According to the
legend: "Not by gold but by the virtue of the leaders was
Namur retaken, 1695."

Emanuel, Elector of Bavaria and Governor of the Spanish Nether-lands. This Wittelsbach prince fought against France in the War of the Grand Alliance (1689-1697) on the side of William III; earlier, he supported the Holy Roman Emperor Leopold I, his father-in-law, against the Turks. His victories in the campaign of 1688 in Southern Hungary and at Belgrade must have especially endeared him to Peter. But after the beginning of the Spanish Succession War in 1701, Maximilian switched to the side of Louis XIV and was driven out of Bavaria.[35] While Peter's refer-ence to Maximilian in a sharply anti-French speech mirrored his-torical reality in 1697 and appeared in both the English and French versions of that year, authors-translators writing after 1701 may have found it anachronistic if not outright embarras-sing as Maximilian became a refugee at the French court and an ally of France. The anonymous biographer of William III who published Peter's speech in 1721 "solved" the problem by call-ing Maximilian, erroneously, "l'Empereur." He thus obfuscated the issue because the only emperor of that name who fought in alliance with England and France (1513) had died two hundred years before and could hardly have been on Peter's mind in 1697. The French version of 1742 printed in a biography of Peter simply omitted the name Maximilian. The clues given in the speech firmly date it to 1697.[35a]

The tsar's Utrecht speech also reveals the psychological urge which drove Peter to Europe and motivated the Great Embassy. The latter's official purpose was to pave the way for a holy alliance of the Christian powers against the Turks. The Embassy's unofficial mission, however, was to acquire and transfer the technological know-how of the West to Muscovy, an enterprise begun earlier[36] but now enhanced by the formidable tsar's curiosity and wish to learn. Throughout the entire trip, the political and technological goals of the mission, Russian state-craft and Peter's personal drive were interlocked.

Some recent writers tend to interpret the Great Embassy as though it had been merely a guise for Peter's naval apprenticeship[37] echoing thereby Burnet's *History of His Own Time* in which the bishop reversed his earlier favorable opinion of Peter preserved in the Thanksgiving sermon. Writing years after the tsar's visit to England which failed to justify the Anglican church leader's exaggerated hopes regarding the possibility of religious reform in Russia, Burnet "concluded for posterity," in Cracraft's words, that Peter "is mechanically turned, and seems designed by nature rather to be a ship-carpenter, than a great prince."[38] Yet Voltaire judged the Great Embassy differently. According to him, "politics had as much of a part in the journey as did instruction."[39] Peter's Utrecht address seems to bear out Voltaire's emphasis on political motivations. The twenty-five-year-old ruler insists, according to the opening sentence of his speech, that it was not the desire to see the "celebrated cities" of the German Empire or of the "most potent" Dutch Republic but rather the "vehement passion" to meet the "Hero of the Age" which made him leave his "throne in a distant country."

Diplomatic flattery alone, so customary on such occasions can only partially explain the tsar's suggestion that from his earliest youth he wished to emulate William's "exploits." Although Peter's close confidant, the Scot General Patrick Gordon was an ardent Jacobite who regarded the Prince of Orange as an usurper, the tsar drank a toast to the health of William upon receiving the news, one year before the Great Embassy left for Europe, that the Jacobite conspiracy against the king had failed.[40] The tsar's openly expressed delight on the occasion of the victory of the joint Anglo-Dutch naval forces at La Hogue over the French prompted the Dutch envoy in Moscow to report in June 1692: "This *young hero* often expresses the lively wish that inspires him, (namely) to join the campaign under the leadership of H.M. King William and participate in the actions against the French or lend his support against them on sea."[41] Bogoslovskii even believed that Peter's adolescent exercises on Pereiaslav Lake should perhaps be considered in the context of the naval operations in the West.[42] Thus, the tsar's admiration for William was sincere and of long standing.

This is not to suggest a simplistic interpretation of the encounter at Utrecht. It was not just Peter's good fortune that "William happened to be in Holland when the Great Embassy arrived."[43] The astute diplomatic maneuverings in which the Great Embassy engaged in the course of its negotiations with Frederick III, Elector of Brandenburg, during the months of May and June 1697, the purposeful combination of political and military pressures to secure a solution favorable to Russia in the then unfolding Polish succession crisis, and the vigorous role played by Peter in these affairs[44] do not justify the assumption of chance as a major factor in interpreting Peter's long desired meeting with William. Nor is it altogether satisfactory to explain that the sudden change in June in the Great Embassy's original travel plans was brought about by the three-year renewal of the defensive-offensive anti-Turkish alliance with the Holy Roman Empire and Venice in Vienna on January 29, this presumably enabling Peter "to go to Holland earlier to learn the art of shipbuilding."[45] The signing of the treaty by his ambassador to the Emperor Leopold I was known to Peter well before the Embassy's departure from Moscow on March 10, if not at the time of writing out, in his own hand, some of the instructions for the Embassy on February 25.[46] While these instructions dealt with much detail of diplomatic etiquette, they failed to mention the most essential, the subject of the negotiations to be conducted by the Embassy in the course of its travels.[47] Whatever the tsar's personal predilections for shipbuilding may have been, these and other technical matters were parts of a political design, and it is in the realm of *haute politique* that we must look for an explanation of the change of course in midstream as the Great Embassy resolved to journey west from Prussia, in the direction of Holland and England, rather than turning sharply south to visit the emperor in Vienna, the pope in Rome, and the doge in Venice, as initially planned.[48] Elements of this decision, executed no doubt on Peter's command, are well known. In the intense competition for the Polish throne, which became vacant in 1696 with the death of the last great national king of Poland, John Sobieski, the two leading candidates were foreigners. One, the Bourbon Prince François Louis Conti, was supported by Louis XIV and hence unacceptable to Peter, who backed the candidacy of Frederick Augustus, Elector of Saxony, a leader of the imperial forces in the anti-Turkish campaigns before the Treaty of Carlowitz (1699). At the time of the Russian negotiations with Brandenburg-Prussia, which also had a stake in the outcome of the elections in Poland, the French candidate's star seemed on the rise, thanks in part to the Francophile sympathies of several Polish Catholic prelates.

The Polish election at the end of June which led to the proclamation of both the Prince Conti and Augustus of Saxony as kings of Poland indicated that Russian concerns were not without foundation.[49] In letters addressed to Polish Cardinal-Primate Michael Stephen Radziejowski, to the Polish senators and the Polish-Lithuanian Commonwealth as well as the king of Denmark, all dated Moscow but in fact dispatched by the Great Embassy from neighboring Prussia, Peter made his views known most emphatically and hardly disguised his intention to intervene militarily if the pro-French faction were to prevail. Reminding the Poles that their country was a member of the anti-Turkish alliance jointly with the Holy Roman Empire, Venice and Moscovy ever since the reign of the late King John III, Peter stressed again and again that the victory of the "French faction" in Poland would endanger Polish statehood and constitute a grave menace to peace. The gist of the argument was that a French prince on the Polish throne would become an ally of the King of France, the traditional supporter of the Turkish Sultan and the Crimean Khan against the cause of Christianity.[50] Setting forth the same reasoning in his letter to the King of Denmark, Peter suggested that his "royal brother" close the Sound, should Conti attempt to reach Poland via the sea route.[51] Ironically, and despite the Danish promise to provide a naval escort for the Great Embassy, Peter was prevented from taking the direct sea route to Holland because Jean Bart, a Dutch privateer in the French service, was rumored to be cruising on the Baltic toward Danzig (Gdansk). Overland, Polish territory had to be avoided since the Poles were deemed to be unstable, especially without a king, and might even launch an attack on the ambassadors.[52]

After watching the unfolding of events in Poland for three weeks from the Prussian city of Pillau, Peter departed on July 11, 1697, "straight for the Dutch land" because, as he put it, his recently renewed alliance with the Emperor was for three years and "there was now nothing to do" in Vienna. He also "fully expected" that after having done "as much as possible" in the Polish elections, of the two kings elected in Poland it was going to be "our king," from Saxony, who was to be crowned in Cracow after converting to the Roman Catholic faith; the emperor and pope would not abandon him either, and nothing more would be heard of the French candidate Conti.[53] Yet en route to Holland, and from there too, even after the conclusion of peace with France at Ryswick, the Great Embassy continued to warn the city of Danzig as well as the Swedes not to give any support to Conti. But although Swedish Chancellor Oxenstierna obliged with 300 cannon for Peter's new Black Sea fleet "for the benefit of all Christianity," as a gesture of good will, Sweden denied any knowledge of the alleged machinations of Prince Conti or any intention to interfere with Polish affairs, and remained neutral till the end of the war.[54]

Thus it was during his trip to Holland that the Muscovite Barbarian and would-be empire builder got his firsthand experience in global politics. To be sure, Russo-French relations were far from cordial in the years before the Great Embassy. Louis XIV's diplomacy toward Muscovy was high-handed and outright hostile. Even during the lifetime of John Sobieski, the French tried to separate Poland, a traditional ally of France since the XVIth century, from the anti-Turkish "Holy League."[55] In Moscow's foreign suburb, there were hardly any Frenchmen, although there was a "Catholic party" at the tsarist court and the Scottish Jacobite General Patrick Gordon was its most influential spokesman. Yet animosity toward France ran high in Moscow and Jesuits trying to travel to China through Muscovite territory were often regarded as French agents.[56] Young Peter also succumbed to the anti-Jesuit fury temporarily, although his nondogmatic religious cynicism prevented him from failing to recognize that Muscovy's anti-Turkish and hence anti-French policies mandated cooperation with the leading Catholic power, the Habsburg Empire and the Papacy.[57]

Russian Francophobia was further formented by the events fo the war fought against Louis XIV in the West. In the course of the campaign, the French navy effectively interrupted foreign shipping with Russia's only seaport, Archangel, in 1696; due to the French blockade of the Northern seaports, not one single Dutch ship was able to reach Muscovy in the summer of that year and Dutch merchant vessels waiting on the high seas were forced to return to Amsterdam. This threatened Russian foreign trade with disaster[58] and also helped Peter understand that Russia's great power status might have to be decided on the battlefields of Western Europe rather than at Azov. The renewed French challenge in Poland added further momentum to his determination to hurry to Holland, in order to be close to the peace negotiations that had commenced in early May 1697, but were far from complete at the time of the Polish crisis in the summer. Above all, Peter desired to meet the architect of the anti-French coalitions who had inspired him for many years, William III.

V

Tobacco Diplomacy and the Russian Card

The Stadholder and King of England was staying at his estate Het Loo near Utrecht when the Great Embassy arrived in Holland in August 1697. To Peter's request for an interview William replied promptly "that he would be with them in 8 days"; the king's emissaries seem to have been in touch with the Russian ambassadors on August 17 and 19. But since Peter, who arrived ahead of the Embassy and spent the week between August 18 and 25 in the Saardam shipyards, joined the Embassy in Amsterdam only on August 26 on the occasion of the latter's ceremonial entry, the meeting of the two monarchs was delayed.[59] One week later, on September 2, Peter sent an agent to The Hague requesting an interview, but this time William needed a breathing spell because of "difficulties in the negotiations with France which tied him down." Within less than a week, however, on September 8, the king's invitation was received; two days later, Peter and his ambassadors boarded a barge which took them overnight to Utrecht.[60]

The sequence of events just indicated does not bear out the contention that William "did not want to complicate matters by meeting with the Tsar of Russia who was advocating a Christian

25

alliance against the Turks who at that time were allies of the French" and hence "a few weeks went by" before the "unofficial" meeting could take place between the two monarchs in the second week of September, by which time "the major issues had been settled at Rijswijk."[61] For while it is true that the negotiations at Ryswick were in a delicate stage when the Russians arrived in Holland and William complained about his "great inquietude, seeing in what a crisis all the affairs of Europe are" on August 28, the crisis was far from over at the time of the Utrecht meeting. Three days after his meeting with Peter, Willima was still "deeply concerned" about the lack of progress in the negotiations with France, and the Earl of Portland, his chief representative, was expected to report to him on September 17; on this same day, the tsar was to meet him for the second time, for a private dinner at Zuylesteyn, near Utrecht. In fact, it is clear from the previous exchanges of Portland and William that they both knew that "we must be prepared to continue the war." This unpleasant alternative may have increased rather than diminished William's desire to meet the tsar, who informed him about another Russian victory over the Turks and Tatars near Azov on the day of Portland's expected arrival.[62]

Peter himself was well informed about the difficulties that blocked the conclusion of peace at Ryswick. One the eve of his departure for Utrecht, he finished a letter to a high ranking official in Moscow by saying that "the French peace has fallen apart" and that "the French were only playing for time as I had said long ago."[63] Indeed to bolster the diplomatic negotiations, the French increased their military and naval pressures in the wake of the opening of peace negotiations in a variety of locations: one French fleet was menacing Boston and New England while another naval force was active in the Spanish Antilles in May. In the Low Lands, French troops advanced on Bruxelles in early June and in August Barcelona, the Catalan capital, surrendered to the forces of Louis XIV following a naval blockade from the sea.[64] In fact, Louis XIV raised his peace terms and insisted on keeping Strasbourg because Leopold I refused to accede to them before the expiration of the August 31 deadline for signing the peace treaty originally agreed upon. It was at that juncture that William sent his invitation to Peter for a conference. Shortly after the Utrecht meeting with the tsar, the king decided to sign the treaty with Louis without the emperor, in view of the British Parliament's and the Dutch Estates' reluctance to continue the war. But he worried about the future and mistrusted French intentions even after the Empire signed the peace with France in late October.[65]

Similarly Peter, challenged once more by Conti in Poland in mid-October, remained suspicious after the final terms of the Ryswick treaty had been completed by the imperial and French ambassadors as shown by his letters to Moscow:

> Peace has been made with the French and for three days there were fireworks in The Hague and here. The fools are very glad, yet the smart ones are not glad because the French cheated, and they expect war [to break out] again soon.[66]

Mistrusting the French, however, did not mean that the tsar "was bitterly disappointed that peace was made."[67] Peace in the West was in Muscovy's best interest because it would liberate the forces of Leopold I, Peter's ally in the Orient, for at least another three years, or so he believed at the time. The chances of obtaining Dutch assistance for his ambitious naval program might also improve with the end of the Nine Years War, although these Russian hopes proved to be unfounded.[68]

Whatever the tsar's personal views of the Treaty of Ryswick,[69] he did not conceal his displeasure with France. While in Holland, the Russian ambassadors were anxious to establish contacts with representatives of all the major powers attending the Congress of Ryswick. But they had strict instructions from Peter not to notify the French diplomats of their arrival: in the words of the secretary of the Great Embassy, "*Moscovie n'a rien à faire avec la France.*"[70] The French records pertinent to the great diplomatic gathering appear to be silent on the activities of the Russians, although the French plenipotentiaries took note of the official reception of the Great Embassy in The Hague.[71]

Strained relations between Paris and Moscow could be traced back to the failure of an ill-informed Russian embassy which proposed an anti-Turkish alliance to France in 1687, when Louis XIV was about to reaffirm his friendship with the traditional Ottoman ally: that mission was also marred by a series of incidents involving the undiplomatic behavior of the Muscovite envoys.[72] The anti-French impulses experienced by Peter in the first period of his active reign mentioned above including his fresh confrontation with Louis XIV over Poland added further momentum to already existing ill feelings. Thus, it is not surprising that the speech he improvised at Utrecht to gain the friendship and support of William III combined elements of youthful admiration for his fellow-monarch with a gallant and apparently sincere offer of aid against France, the mutual foe.

In his speech, the tsar did not mention Poland, the most recent and still acute area of Franco-Muscovite conflict. He may have refrained from doing so because two weeks earlier, on the day of his arrival in Amsterdam, he learned from the report of his permanent envoy in Warsaw, Aleksei Nikitin, that Augustus of Saxony had converted to the Catholic faith, arrived in Cracow, and was about to be crowned King of Poland. With the same mail, Peter received confirmation from Moscow of the, for him, favorable turn of events in Poland.[73] It is nevertheless interesting that according to the report of the ambassador of the Polish-Saxon king Augustus, he was informed by William and not by Peter that Polish affairs had been discussed at the Utrecht encounter and that the tsar was about to dispatch 60,000 troops to the Lithuanian border to assist Augustus.[74] It is noteworthy that under the date of September 17, Luttrell's *Diary* refers not only to William's private dinner with Peter and the latter's new victories over the Turks, but also to an alleged report

> From Warsaw, that 60,000 Muscovites were drawing towards the frontiers of Poland to favour the coronation of the elector of Saxony, and that the crown of Sweden had also promised his assistance; and several gentlemen, thought to have been in the French interest, now favour the elector.[75]

The passage just quoted is far from unique. Since the fall of 1696 when Conti was reported to have "mortgaged his estates for 600,000 livres" preparing for Poland "where he stands fair to be chose king at the election appointed to be held there in May next,"[76] the British followed the steps of the French prince and his party closely. Along with news of the military situation in the West, Luttrell meticulously registered the fortunes of the imperial forces and their Hungarian and Turkish opponents in the Danubian theater, the events of the Polish Diet and the activities of "the czar of Muscovy" at the Prussian court in May and June 1697.[77] Between mid-June and mid-August, news of the attempts of British and Dutch naval forces to keep the ships of the French privateer Bart locked up in Dunkirk (because the latter's "design was to sail for Dantzik, to have influenc'd Conti's election in Poland") alternated with news of the seizure of "a small sea port in Prussia" by "the French party" in Poland "where they expect Conti with Du Bart's squadron" and of Danish efforts "to hinder Du Barts passing the Sound to transport forces to Conti's assistance in Poland." At the same time, Luttrell reports "great likelyhood of an alliance between Moscovy, Denmark, and Brandenburgh" together with the defeat of the Hungarian anti-Habsburg insurgents, the progress made by Augustus II in Poland and the first friendly contacts between William and Peter in Holland.

These reports may have been colored by wishful thinking, as was the case with the tsar's "designs to embrace the protestant religion, and set up an university at Moscow," but they did contain elements of truth and occasionally reflected a mutuality of interests that ultimately prevailed, if not at the first encounter of William and Peter, then when the latter visited England.

This happened in the case of a request of "Our Virginia merchants here," who upon hearing about William's forthcoming interview with the tsar,

> . . . have sent over some persons on their behalf to lay before the king the great advantages that may accrue to this nation in case his majestie can prevail with the czar to permit the importation of tobacco to Muscovy, which hitherto has been prohibited.[78]

Indeed, before Peter had even set foot on Dutch soil, "tobacco diplomacy" came into play. On July 25, 1697 William Blathwayt, secretary in attendance on William III in Holland, advised Secretary of State William Trumbull to use the tsar's forthcoming visit to the king "to Obtain Some Advantage in Trade or at least the Restoring Our Former Privileges from the good Nature of the Czar, when We shall have made much of him."[79] In the following weeks, members of the old Muscovy Company, London merchants and traders to Virginia and Maryland vied with each other in making recommendations to the Board of Trade, which forwarded them to the Lords Justices who in turn sent the report to the attention of the king without delay so he could seize "the opportunity of the Czar's coming into Holland, to procure for English merchants some of the advantages proposed. . . ."[80]

The British proposals suggested the restoration of the privileges granted to English traders in the sixteenth and seventeenth centuries but withdrawn in 1648. These included "liberty to come with their ships. . . to any port of that Empire" [i.e., Muscovy], "liberty to trade within all that Empire inwards and outwards. . . without paying any manner of customs, tolls, or duties whatsoever. . . " and "liberty to travel to and to reside and trade in what places they think fit; as also to transport their goods to and from Persia and other places custom free through the Russian Empire." In case of a Russian refusal, the British envoys would then ask for a reduction of customs, and assurances "that they shall be entitled to whatsoever privileges may at any time hereafter be granted to others. . . ." Above all, the British wanted the tsar's permission to import tobacco, owing to "the extent of those territories, the number of the people, and their passionate love of tobacco."[81]

By the second half of August, the English plenipotentiaries at Ryswick had instructions

> to welcome the Czar or his Ambassadors on their arrival at The Hague, and to endeavour to procure for the King's subjects such privileges as they formerly enjoyed, and such further privileges as they now desire; assuring the Czar of the King's strict friendship and his desire for mutual benefits of trade between their subjects.[82]

Writing to Secretary Trumbull from The Hague on August 23, Matthew Prior, the secretary to the British Embassy and Delegation at Ryswick thought that "If the Czar pleases to honour us with a visit, His Majesty will likewise come for a day or two, and I hope he will not be further from us than Loo till the great business is perfected." Three weeks later, he registered the two main themes discussed by William and Peter at their first personal encounter:

> The King has seen the Czar of Muscovy *incognito* at Utrecht. The immediate use we endeavour to make of him is that he would allow tobacco to be imported into his dominions, which has been forbid since the year '48. His own inclinations oblige him to carry on a war with the Turk, and for that purpose to get a fleet ready for the Black Sea. He is absolutely against the French, and that aversion may contribute a good deal towards settling the crown of Poland upon the Elector of Saxony.

In the same context, Prior also noted that "The Prince of Conti is parted from Dunkirk, we say, with a squadron of John de Bart's commanding from Dunkirk though I have seen good advices from France which say he is gone privately by land, and that only his followers are embarked *pour sauver les apparences.* It is certain," he added, that Conti's party "is stronger than was thought, and that the Elector wants money, the needful qualifications toward succeeding in a Polish Diet."[83]

Although we do not have Prior's letter to Undersecretary of State John Ellis, which "relates the interview the King has had with the Czar," another letter tells us that William was "very well pleased with him and invited him to dinner."[84] In view of the significance of trade, especially tobacco trade, and the multiplicity of expectations and pressures, commercial, cultural-religious, political and military, which began to build up in the summer of 1697 suggesting the desirability of negotiations with Muscovy, the last paragraph of Peter's Utrecht speech promising to grant the British "greater Immunities than ever they Yet had," must have contributed to the king's satisfaction.

There are certain parallels between the British perception of a volatile European scene which included the eastern half of the continent, and the intentions and attitudes of the tsar, anxious to play a role on that same stage. On the very day he registered the Virginia merchants' interest in exporting tobacco to Muscovy, Luttrell also remarked that "the king had sent to compliment the tsar of Muscovy at Nimeghen, and the states have ordered their governours to salute him with a discharge of the cannon thro' those places which he shall passe as he comes to the Hague." Two days earlier, less than a fortnight before the Utrecht meeting, another entry informs us that "the prince of Baden, by the emperor's order, was to march the 19th (of August, O.S.) with 5 imperial regiments to Hungary . . . . Dubart has orders immediately to put to sea, but 22 English and Dutch men of war lye before Dunkirk to keep him in. The Muscovites, it's said have taken the province of Precop from the Tartars" and "60,000 Muscovites are arrived on the frontiers of Poland to invade that kingdom, in case they insist on Conty's election." Items about the Hungarian rebels, unruly Poles and the Muscovite tsar's moves continue to intermingle, occasionally in a most dramatic way, as when on the eve of "the enterview between his majestie and the czar" it was learned that "the prince of Conty was sailed from Dunkirk to Poland, carrying with him 4 millions of livres and many experienced officers; but 'tis thought the elector of Saxony will be crowned by his party before the others arrival." That "Conti embark'd on the 6th (O.S.) for Dantzik" was reported along with the first encounter between William and Peter; the abstract of the articles of peace "between king William and the French king, as they are already agreed to by France, which were to be signed to morrow", i.e., on September 20, was received with the news that "Dubart, with his squadron, is past the Sound, with Conti on board, for Dantzick."[85]

The crisis around Danzig and Poland continued well beyond the peace of Ryswick, and the British could not remain indifferent to it. Strangely enough, their reaction to it reflected on occasion the language used by the tsar in his letters as shown by an entry advising that

> 30,000 men at Warsaw have protested against crowning *our elector,* declared him an enemy to Poland, and those rebels who adhere to him; Conty's party have got the body of the deceased king into their possession, which according to the lawes of the countrey ought to be buried before another is crowned; however *his majestie is resolved to abide the extremity.* [86]

Given William's mistrust of Louis XIV, the anti-Turkish campaigns of both emperor and tsar in the Balkans and the Black Sea region, and the protracted Polish succession crisis that carried into the new century when two additional generations of Princes Conti received French support,[87] there seemed to be room for British-Russian cooperation in the international arena.

Hence Peter's offer couched in such romantic terms at Utrecht was appreciated by William, and since the dynastic and state interests of both monarchs demanded a "Saxon" solution to the Polish question in preference to French designs, the contours of the first Anglo-Russian "entente cordial" were drawn over East Central Europe. Rumors went even further in early October, suggesting "a new alliance between the kings of England, Sweden, and Denmark, the states general, the electors of Brandenburgh and Hanouer, the czar, &c., and the Switzers and the city of Geneva will be included."[88]

Russian participation in European affairs, with an anti-French accent, was very much in the air for many months after Ryswick, and indeed for years. Writing a generation later, Voltaire still had a keen sense of this. An admirer of the Sun King and of the tsar, whose daughter, the Empress Elizabeth, commissioned his history of Russia,[89] he was reluctant to write a biography of Peter because he did not want to discuss the tsar's private life, his shortcomings and fits of rage, only the accomplishments that survive him, so that the book would contibute "equally to the glory of Peter I, his daughter the Empress & his nation."[90]

Voltaire's willingness to "suppress" historical evidence and to be highly selective for the sake of a certain cause acquires particular significance because to him, Peter was one of the "Great Men" who were the true makers of history and captured the imagination of contemporaries and posterity alike. For thirty years, as he himself put it, he was fascinated by the tsar; although he began to think of writing about Peter in 1737, he requested a book about him from a friend as early as 1729.[91] While he permitted himself to be manipulated by Catherine the Great, Voltaire used Peter's example and his presumed legacy to prove that whereas French civilization was on the decline since the death of Louis XIV, Russia continued to rise under the enlightened government of Catherine. But even before he became the propagandist of the "Semiramis of the North" ready to justify her expansionism as "crusades for Enlightenment,"[92]

Voltaire's Russophilism, in sharp contrast to the Russophobia of Louis XV,[93] asserted itself in more than one way. Three examples are particularly relevant to our theme.

In his magisterial study on *The Age of Louis XIV,* first published in 1751, Voltaire discussed the Polish elections of June 1697. Claiming that although Conti was elected first by the majority of the estates and proclaimed King of Poland by the primate, Augustus of Saxony, elected by a minority two days later, had his troops ready on the frontier. Prince Conti was absent from the scene, "without money, without troops, without power;" the French government's financial and military support was inadequate. Upon his arrival in Danzig, Conti ran into opposition. "The intrigues of the pope and the emperor, the money and the troops of Saxony had already assured the crown to his rival. He returned with the glory of having been elected. France was mortified by revealing that she did not have sufficient strength to provide a king for Poland."

While Voltaire placed part of the blame for Conti's "disgrace" on Louis XIV, who should either have prevented the prince from accepting the crown offered to him, or should have given him adequate support to prevail,[94] the role played by Peter and Russia are conspicuously missing from this account. The Polish elections are presented as a sideshow of Ryswick and the tsar is mentioned only in connection with the Northern War, as the reformer and founder of his empire.[95]

In the first part of his *History of the Russian Empire under Peter the Great,* which went to press in 1759, less than a decade after the *Age of Louis XIV,* Voltaire suggests that the double nomination of Conti and Augustus was "confirmed" to Peter in Saardam six weeks after the event, admitting, however, that upon receiving the news, "the carpenter of Saardam immediately promised thirty thousand men to King Augustus."[96] This error is the more astonishing because he must have known from the manuscript of Lefort about the timing and extent of the Muscovite "involvement" in the affairs of Poland. From the same manuscript, he also learned that the Russian ambassadors exchanged visits with all of the ambassadors attending the Ryswick congress except with those of France, whom they failed to notify, in Voltaire's words, "not only because the tsar took the side of King Augustus against the Prince Conti, but because King William, whose friendship he cultivated, did not want peace with France at all."[97]

This account, of course, did not quite correspond to the historical facts. Nor can such a series of interlocking misinterpretations be entirely unintentional. Whereas in his work on the age of Louis he chose to suppress Peter's participation in the confirmation of Augustus, Voltaire's partial admission of the Russian role in his book glorifying Peter was an attempt to absolve the latter from all anti-Polish wrongdoing by insinuating that the "Carpenter of Saardam" was *procul negotiis,* and insofar as he was not removed from worldly affairs, he fell victim to his youthful uncritical adulation of William, the real culprit responsible for both Muscovy's Francophobia and for the sabotaging of the peace negotiations.

There are two interlocking aspects of Voltaire's presentation and the information gathered from Russian and British sources regarding the unfolding of events after the Polish "double election" of 1697. Both contestants accused the other of having resorted to bribery on a massive scale and both are probably right. Electoral corruption coupled with violence was an ancient custom in Poland and the elections of 1697 constituted no exception. But the failure of Conti's Polish adventure cannot be explained by the absence of adequate French financial, military and political means from the local scene as stated by Voltaire. Celebrated in a poem by the son of the "great" Conti who became a candidate for the Polish throne, Voltaire was very close to the princely family of the Contis.[98] He must have been aware of the ambiguity of the relationship between Louis XV and the "great" Conti who had fought with the imperial forces in Hungary against the Turk in defiance of his king in the mid-1680's;

Voltaire often praised the charming personality of the prince.[99] He must also have known that the grandson of the "great" Conti, prince Louis François, who participated in both the Polish and Austrian wars of succession (1733-35 and 1740-48, respectively), was also a candidate for the Polish crown supported by Louis XV's secret diplomacy.[100] It may well be that it was exactly Voltaire's intimate knowledge of the political maneuvers behind the Polish candidacies of the two Conti princes, both of which had failed, that motivated him to ignore the larger questions the historian must ask.

Bishop Burnet's History of His Own Times, the 1724 London edition of which was in the library at Ferney and which Voltaire quotes in letters as far apart as 1740 and 1761,[101] a period during which he wrote his *Age of Louis XIV* and *History of Russia under Peter the Great,* raises these larger issues in the context of the major events of the year 1697. After surveying the domestic developments in England and the Allied military-naval struggle against the French in Flanders, the Iberian peninsula and the West Indies, Burnet analyzes at length the "great change of affairs" in Poland including the contest for the crown. Then he turns to the tsar's "great designs" and his travel to Holland and England, "A very unusual accident. . . that served not a little to his [Augustus's] quiet establishment on the throne of Poland." According to Burnet, the tsar "might be forced to have a share" in a war resulting from the dispute over Poland because he

> concerned himself much in the matter, not only by reason of the neighbourhood, but because he feared, that if the French party should prevail, France being in an alliance with the Turk, a king sent from thence would probably not only make a peace with the Turk, but turn his arms against himself, which would hinder all his designs for a great fleet.[102]

Concluding his summary of the Russian view of Poland, Burnet added that since "the French party was strongest in Lithuania,"

Peter brought "a great army to the frontier of that duchy, to be ready to break into it, if a war should begin in Poland: and we were told, that the terror of this had a great effect."

As to the fate of Conti, the bishop described how the prince managed to elude "a squadron of ours" that kept him locked up at Dunkirk for some time, only to land at Marienburg because Danzig refused to permit him to bring along his entire force. Dwelling on Conti's tribulations in the Baltic area, Burnet mentions that the prince hesitated to distribute all the money he had brought from France among the leaders of his party and that he "would not trust the Poles." Referring to Conti's ultimate return to Dunkirk and the papal court's rejoicing "at the pretended conversion of the new king," namely, Augustus, Burnet justifies his detailed account by concluding:

> This may prove of such importance, both to the political and religious concerns of Europe, that I thought it deserved that a particular mention should be made of it, though it lies at a great distance from us: it had some influence in disposing the French now to be more earnest for a peace; for if they had a king of Poland in their dependance, that would have given them a great interest in the northern parts, with an easier access, both to assist the Turk and the malecontents in Hungary.[103]

What Burnet's contemporary history suggests clearly confirms the Polish-American historian Oscar Halecki's observation according to wich the establishment of a branch of the French dynasty in Poland, after the weakening of France's two other traditional allies, Sweden and Turkey, in the last decades of the seventeenth century, "would have changed the whole balance of power in Europe to the advantage of Louis XIV."[104]

In his *Age of Louis XIV,* Voltaire therefore placed a special emphasis on England's desire to maintain a balance of power on the European continent and among its dynasties.[105] Yet in his analysis of the Polish events of 1697 he ignored the complementary roles of Muscovy and England in their efforts to prevent

France from upsetting the British concept of that European balance which he himself perceived. The giant of the Enlightenment, who regarded his history of Peter "the confirmation and supplement of" his history of Charles XII and insisted that his work on Louis XIV was "composed without interest, without fear and without hope, by a man whom his circumstances placed in a position of flattering no one"[106] was neither above flattering the powerful or immune to flattery by them.[107] While quoting the opinion of the ex-king of Poland, Stanislas Leszczynski, as proof of his correct interpretation of the events set forth in his study on Charles XII,[108] Voltaire was certainly not oblivious to the fact that Leszczynski's daughter happened to have married Louis XV, and thus was Queen of France. Nor could he ignore the radical change in the balance of power which was in progress at the time of writing his history of Peter. After century-long struggles, Bourbon and Habsburg fought side-by-side in the Seven Years' War and both were allied with Russia against the Anglo-Prussian partnership.

Voltaire may have seen incipient Franco-Russian cooperation on the battlefield and in diplomacy in the wake of the reversal of alliances in 1756 as an overdue completion of the unfinished Petrine legacy forty years after the tsar's visit to Paris. An admirer of Peter, and anxious to be of service to his daughter, the Empress Elizabeth, Voltaire himself wished to be and actually became an important cultural link between Russia and France. While promoting a better understanding between the two countries, he tended to close his eyes to the Anglo-Russian entente aspired to by Peter sixty years before. Under these conditions, Peter's anti-French rhetoric and anti-Polish deeds of 1697 were both anachronistic and inopportune to Voltaire. This is why he found no use for the 1697 French text of Peter's Utrecht speech: at best, he thought it to be another propaganda sheet in the ongoing war of nerves between Louis XIV and William III. As far as the printed French version goes, Voltaire may not have been

far from the truth. But the speech was not only propaganda although it may have been intended for that use by the British
once they resolved that they might use the "Russian card" on
the eve of Ryswick and thereafter if circumstances necessitat-
ed it.

3. Medal commemorating the Utrecht meeting of William III and Peter I in 1697. Courtesy Penrose Library, Rare Book Collection, University of Denver, Denver, Colorado. Source: *The Metalic History of the Three Last Reigns: Or a Series of Medals, representing all the Remarkable Events from the Revolution, to the Death of King George I*, Plate XXII, no. 4 and p. 38. Included in vol. IV (1744) of *The History of England*. Written in French by Mr. Rapin de Thoyras. Translated into English with additional notes by N. Tindal. 2d ed., 4 vols. (London, 1732–47). The front represents the king's bust crowned with laurel and this legend:

GULIELM[US]III D[E]G[RATIA]M[AGNAE]BRIT[ANNIAE]FR[ANCIAE]ET HIB[ERNIAE,

GULIELM[US] III D[EI] G[RATIA] M[AGNAE] BRIT[ANNIAE] FR[ANCIAE] ET HIB[ERN.- X
F[IDEI] D[EFENSOR] P[IUS] A[UGUSTUS] (William III, by the Grace of God, King of Great Britain, France and Ireland, defender of the faith, pious, august).

The reverse shows the king receiving the Tsar at the gate of his palace, with these words in the rim: SIC OLIM HEROES (thus [acted] once the heroes). In the background, the city of Utrecht. In the exergue the following inscription: PETRI ALEXIEWICZ CZAR MAGNIQVE GULIELMI REGIS AMICITIA TRAIECTI AD RHEN[UM] XI SEPTEMB[RIS] MDCXCVII NC (The friendship of Tsar Peter Alexievich and the great King William, brought to the Rhine, September 11, 1697). Cf. pp. 9 and 17 above and Appendix no. 4.

PETER THE GREAT.

4. Peter the Great. From a print by I. Smith after a painting by Sir Godfrey
Kneller. Courtesy Library of Congress, Washington, D. C. Cf. p. 50 below.

5. William III. Reproduction of a painting by Sir Godfrey Kneller. Courtesy Library of Congress, Washington, D. C.

6. French account of the first encounter between William III and Peter I at Utrecht. Courtesy Bibliothèque Public et Universitaire, Geneva, Switzerland. Département des manuscrits, Cote Ms. F. 1013, p. 63. Cf. pp. 65-66 below and n.174.

Les Bourgmaistre Witzen & Presidents . . . .
& Les deux Pensionnaires qui Les auoyent com=
plimentés, & apres Eux Suiuoyent Jn Cortege -
de quarante Carosse & vne nombreuse Caualcade
de gentils hommes qui Les accompagnerent jusq́
dans Leur Hostel.

uant que de prendre audience des Estats Generaux
il allerent a Utrech auec Le Czaar enuiron Le -
10e de 7bre où ils Se rendirent Le matin. Sa
majté Britanniq̄ß Sy rendit trois heures apres
& descendit a Lauberge où Le Czaar estoit -
Logé. Les Ambassadeurs moscouits allerent
dés aussy tost complimenter Le Roy Guillaume
dans Sa Chambre. Le General Le Fort qui portoit
La parole apres quelques entretiens proposa -
a S. m. B. Si Elle nauroit pas pour agreable -
De voir Le Czaar qui estoit dans La Chambre
prochaine. Le Roy Layant agreé y passa auec -
huit personnes, Les deux Princes en Se Saluant
Se prirent La main en signe d'amitié, Leur
conuersation roula Sur Les affaires de Pologne,
& Sur La paix qui Se traictoit a Ruiswik; apres
S'estre donné des marques reciproques d'affection
Le Czaar offrit du vin au Roy, Lequel le remercia
Le Roy a Son tour inuita Le Czaar a disner, -
mais quoy quil Leut comme accepté il S'en -
excusa Sur Le Champ disant quil Seroit veu de
trop de monde. Le Roy Sortit tres Satisfait &
fort joyeux de cette conference qui fust assis -
Longue & dont Le General Le Fort fust seul
Linterprete. Le Roy trouua Le Czaar bien
fait & dun raisonnem̄ solide.

mme Le Czaar ne voulut point estre connu, Les
Gazetiers de Holande eurent ordre de ne point -
parler de S. m. Cz. mais vni quem̄ des Ambassad̄
moscouites ce qui fust bien observé; Cependant
Les Holandois qui voyageoyent & negocioyent -
a Moscou Layans reconnu quoy quil S'habilla

Entrevûe du Czaar
& du Roy Guillaum
a Utrecht.

Les Gazetiers d'Hole
ont ordre de ne pt fai
mention du Czaar

VI

Technology Transfer and the Balance of Power in East Central Europe

Viewed against the historical background described above, the "Czar of Muscovy's speech to King William when he met him at Utrecht" is a most remarkable document, revealing the more ambitious aims of a young ruler bent on imperial expansion. Aside from articulating the idea of an Anglo-Russian alliance directed against France, the speech also formulated, the first time, Russian great power ambitions in a West European context at a time when neither the Maritime Powers, nor France seemed to be prepared to regard Muscovy as a partner of equal standing in the international arena. Yet this only adds to the tension and fascination inherent in the historical moment of the two monarchs' encounter.

To be sure, Peter's capture of Azov and his subsequent visit to England led to the British observation that "Russia might play some part in limiting French influence in Eastern Europe."[109] But there were no regular diplomatic contacts between Muscovy and England at the time, and it took several years before the first exchange of British and Russian permanent envoys occurred.[110] Peter's resentment of the French, noted with

41

delight by the British, and the Great Embassy's isolation from the French representatives, although in part a legacy of the Muscovite past, were nevertheless limitations of Russia's diplomatic maneuvering possibilities. Moreover the hopes, also reflected in the speech, that the Swedish control of Russia's northern trade might be broken by relying on the Maritime Powers proved to be unrealistic because Sweden's military might was an important factor in the calculations of William III and his successors in the event of a renewal of hostilities with France, as the Great Northern War and the Spanish War of Succession were to show.[111]

Although shifts in world affairs were to cause Peter to alter his short-range plans in the Black Sea region and to modify Russia's relations with other great powers in years to come, his determination to secure great power status for his country in the Baltic and East Central Europe, seen during the Polish succession crisis, and his vision of Russia's global role manifest in the trip of the Great Embassy, and spelled out with a measure of romantic eloquence in his speech at Utrecht, remained. Delivered perhaps as an informal toast, the speech permits a rare insight into the thinking of the twenty-five-year-old ruler. The four variants of what could be called the "imperial idea" in the five short paragraphs of the tsar's statement contain an important message.

In his opening words Peter addressed William as ("most renowned") "emperor" although his concluding expression of esteem clearly revealed his awareness of the British monarch's royal title ("worthiest of kings"). This discrepancy was no mere oversight. The tsar had just concluded some delicate negotiations with Brandenburg, an important part of which revolved around the elector's desire, reflected in the duly signed treaty, to receive Russian assistance in attaining royal status among the rulers of Europe.[112] Peter also knew that the German lands constituted an empire, but the language in which he referred to it lacked precision ("German" instead of "Holy Roman Empire"). Such casual handling of the imperial theme suggests not only the improvised nature of the speech befitting an informal occasion: Peter and members of his retinue, which included a number of translators and other experts, had sufficient time to prepare a draft observing stricter diplomatic protocol, as shown by many official documents addressed to foreign dignitaries by the Great Embassy. "Looseness" in the Utrecht speech was neither accidental nor without purpose.

Two caveats must be considered at this point. We know from the seventeenth-century diary of Patrick Gordon, who was in the Russian service, that the tsar was often referred to in English as "the Emperour of Russia" and "his Imperiall Majestie of Russia."[113] Luttrell's *Diary,* however, shows that in England proper the term "czar of Moscovy" prevailed at the time.[114] Be that as it may, Peter spoke no English and the word he used in his speech was in all likelihood "Keizer" just as he would address in Dutch, Prince F. Y. Romodanovskii as "Min Her Koni(c)h" (My Lord King) in many of his own handwritten Russian letters even before arriving in Holland.[115]

Further, since the early sixteenth century, European royalty, including kings of both England and France continued using the title "emperor-empereur" in reference to the tsar of Muscovy in diplomatic correspondence, although the title "empereur" was replaced by "czar" in French diplomacy upon the order of Louis XIV in 1668. As has been pointed out, however, such liberal handling of the imperial title did not necessarily imply the free-wheeling transfer of the imagery and symbolism inherent in the office of the "Imperator" of the West, but rather the insinuation of the exotic nature of certain potentates such as the rulers of China or Tartary.[116] Yet when Peter decided to address the King of England as "emperor," it was precisely the idea of greeting in William the leader of the West, equal in rank to the Holy Roman Emperor, their joint ally, and to the "universal" monarch of France, their common enemy. In addition to making a skillful gesture of *captatio benevolentiae* toward his host in Utrecht, the tsar of Muscovy instinctively, but not without calculation, also meant to heighten his own stature by insisting at the end of the second paragraph of his speech that it was his "imperial" model, the true military leader of the anti-French coalition in the West who "Instilled into my Breast the first thoughts I had of Enlarging my Dominions," i.e., building an empire in the East of Europe.[117]

The emperor-to-be of the East thus visualized the coexistence of a maritime empire in the west with the Holy Roman Empire in the middle of the continent and his own yet to be effectuated. And if he began his short address by paying tribute to the "Most Renowned Emperor"'s "Martial Genious," which he claimed had inspired his own military breakthrough at Azov, then the allusion to his own enlarged dominions was symbolically rounded out in the last paragraph with a reference to "My Empire" by adding an emphasis on shipping and trade, the lasting foundations of global power.

Incidentally, the war against the Ottoman Empire is not specifically mentioned beyond the modest reference to his own victories at the beginning of Peter's brief address. Although Peter was looking for new allies in addition to the ones he had already enlisted against the Turk, namely, Venice, the Holy Roman Empire and Poland, the Great Embassy was extremely cautious when it came to the sealing of a new agreement, as shown by the wording of the June alliance with Brandenburg; while the promotion of trade between the two countries took a prominent place in the text, any reference that could have affected the delicate balance of Northeastern Europe by upsetting the Swedes was confined to verbal understandings and confirmed only by a handshake of the tsar and the elector.[118] Similarly, it would have been unrealistic of Peter to expect William "to join him in a Christian alliance against the Turks," as has been suggested.[119] The tsar knew that it was not in the interest of the Maritime Powers to expand, let alone get directly into, the oriental war which would weaken the forces available to contain France. Hence his Utrecht address formulated the idea of an anti-French Anglo-Russian alliance, the first of its kind, coupling it with the offer to strengthen Anglo-Dutch trade with those northern provinces of his realm which were threatened not only by the French during the hostilities but also by the Swedes, who attempted to transform the Baltic into a Swedish lake.[120]

Thus, Peter's speech, indirectly, was also aimed at Sweden without mentioning that country by name. Such an interpretation tends to corroborate the views of Hatton and Wittram who cite Swedish and French reports suggesting that during his visits to Holland and England, the tsar openly expressed his intention to acquire a port on the Baltic.[121] It should also be remembered that at the time, Archangel, "a most important link in British-Muscovite trade relations since the sixteenth century," was Russia's only outlet to the sea and that Peter perceived foreign trade as "one of the vehicles of Russia's involvement in Europe and one of the natural channels of European influence upon the subsequent changes within Russian society."[122] In fact, the Utrecht speech is an early proof of the interrelationship of political objectives and economic means in Peter's thinking. It also supports Hatton's opinion regarding the role of Russia's "window toward the west," a concept which "was shaping in the Tsar's head under the stimulus of his first tour of Europe: a Muscovy in direct contact with the great trading powers would become a modern Russia. . . ."[123]

But beyond revealing some of Peter's boldest dreams of Russia's role among the nations of the world, the timing of the speech was most significant from William's point of view. Its offer of friendship came when peace with France, albeit in reaching distance, might nevertheless elude William in the last moment, in which case, even for bargaining purposes, it was advantageous to have Russia as a potential new ally. The fact

that William was anxious to meet with Peter once he reached
Holland is as significant as the tsar's longstanding and ardent
wish for this personal encounter. To be sure, hopes that former
British privileges in Muscovy might be restored and even extended for the tobacco trade, so that the British could vend "our
tobacco through their vast dominions, which would be of the
greatest importance to England and the plantations," failed to
materialize during the negotiations in Holland although William's
ambassadors at The Hague had "very full instructions to treat
with the Czar and his ambassadors."[124] In their note addressed
to Lefort in October, 1697, the English plenipotentiaries Lord
Pembrock, Villiers and Williamson stated that earlier than any
other people in Europe, the British had established friendly and
mutually advantageous commercial relations with Russia; they
proposed a renewal of the old alliances and the century-long
friendship. The Muscovite delegation, however, refrained from
committing itself while listening to proposals of various groups
of English merchants. Peter postponed the decision until his
visit to England. When the contract was finally signed shortly
before his departure from Britain in early April, 1698, it neither
restored the Muscovy Company's old privileges, nor permitted
the free trade requested by the Virginia merchants. The tobacco
monopoly was granted to the Marquess of Carmarthen and his
associates for a period of two-to-seven years in return for a
much needed advance payment of £12,000 to the tsar when he
was still in London.[125]

The preferential treatment received by the Marquess of Carmarthen over his competitors can be traced to the aftermath of
the first personal meeting between William and Peter, which
marked the auspicious prelude to the tsar's subsequent trip to
England, where Carmarthen became his travelling companion
upon the king's instructions. For even though it has been con-
templated before, Peter's journey to the island country was
given additional momentum by the encounter at Utrecht, which

laid the foundation for further personal contacts between the two rulers and was followed by additional courtesies extended to the tsar by his royal host. One may add that whatever reservations the king may have expressed in private regarding the strange habits and uncouth attire of his Muscovite guest,[126] William "went out of his way to be a considerate host."[127]

Undoubtedly, Peter's admiration couched in such lyrical terms at Utrecht and the tsar's anti-French bias must have appealed to the king. Often accused of being cold and taciturn and never fully recovered from the shock of his wife's death,[128] William III could not have been expected to reciprocate in kind the effusive words of the young giant of Muscovy although the "kind embraces" mentioned in Peter's address and by Luttrell[129] testify to the cordial atmosphere of the first encounter between the two monarchs. Nor do the friendly gestures with which William followed up his first meeting with the tsar leave any doubt that he intended to retain Peter's support and goodwill.

Six weeks after the Utrecht meeting, and even before summarizing the tsar's speech, Luttrell noted in his diary that "The king continues still at Loo, and has presented the czar of Moscovy with the Royal Transport yatch, being the best sailer we had; and 'tis now said again he will accompany his majestie for England some time next month. . . ."[130] Interestingly, the "leak" on which Luttrell's entry was based preceded by almost a month the official letter with which Lord Carmarthen, the designer of the ship, notified Peter of William's generous and unexpected gift.[131] It may be noted, further, that Lord Carmarthen's letter written upon William's instructions immediately after the latter's return to England specifically refers to the tsar as "the defender of the Christian faith" who fought so valiantly "against the *common enemy*, the Turk and the Crimean khan."[132] Six weeks earlier and shortly after William had signed the Ryswick treaty with Louis XIV, Luttrell speculated that "Some of our troops are to goe into the emperors service against the Turks, and his ambassadors at The Hague are treating with the czar about a close alliance between them, in order to carry on the war to Constantinople."[133] Indeed a "Congratulatory Poem" welcoming the tsar on his arrival in England in January, 1698, called "the High and Mighty Czar of Muscovy" and "the Great Nassaw" "the greatest Men the World can Shoe" because the "powerful Work" of these "Twins of Fate. . . . Subdues both Mahomet and the Christian Turk," namely, the King of France. Exhorting the tsar to "Go on, Great Sir, pursue thy great Design," the unknown author neatly assigns complementary roles to Peter and William by referring to the former's "Glist'ning Sabre" which gleams on "proud Asia" and dazzles "Frighted *Tarters*":

> Its Conquering Steel shall to the *East* give Law,
> Whilst NASSAW's Scepter keeps the *West* in Awe.[134]

Echoing some of the imagery contained in the poem dedicated to Amsterdam Burgomaster Witsen on the occasion of the Utrecht meeting between William and Peter,[135] the ode likens Peter to a "travelling Phoebus" gilding Britain by its beams on its way while compelling the East to adore the "Rising Sun." It ends with the wish:

> May Roman Conquest be out done by Thee
> And CZAR to more than CAESAR then extended Be.

The baroque language of the poem, printed at the end of March, 1698 (O.S.), suggests that at least certain segments of the English public attributed political-military significance to the tsar's visit. Traces of this can be detected in Bishop Burnet's Thanksgiving sermon at Whitehall in December of the previous year. The curiosity with which the British press anticipated Peter's arrival and followed his steps in England, the speculations and rumors registered along with official reports in Luttrell's

Diary point in the same direction: the first information of early August, 1697, that "The czar of Moscovy is come to Leewarden, in East Freezland, within 2 days of Loo," and William and Peter are about to meet, is followed by the statement "'tis believed he will accompany his majestie to England." The report about the royal present of the yacht to the tsar six weeks later precedes an interesting association of expectations and news items:

> . . . and 'tis now said again he will accompany his majestie for England some time next month, by which time the French will have quitted the Spanish garrisons in Flanders [i.e., in accordance with the agreements of Ryswick just concluded].
> The divisions in Poland continue to encrease; that 700 horse of Conty's party have possest themselves of Marienburgh, stileing him the protector of their liberties.

In early November, "It is still said the czar of Moscovy will come over with his majestie," in the middle of the month, "Here is a report that the czar of Moscovy came over hither incognito with the earl of Portland, and that he went with his lordship the other day to see Windsor castle. . . . 5 foreigners were at the Tower to see the rarities there. . . the officers had instructions not to take any money of them: some will have that they were Russians, and the czar among them." At the end of November, "Most people are of opinion that the czar of Moscovy is here incognito, and the rather, for that sir John Wolfe, one of the last sherifs, who were acquainted with him in Moscow, and understands the language, was absent at the cavalcade on Tuesday." Again, in late December, "Sir John Wolfe attended 3 Muscovites, and shewed them the lords and commons as they were sitting; one of them was in a green vest, richly lined with furr, supposed to be the czar."[136]

A month later, in January, 1698, Peter arrived in England on board of the Yorke, flagship of Vice-Admiral Sir David Mitchell's naval squadron. Towns and warships passed by the squadron fired salutes and a similar royal escort took the

departing tsar back to Holland at the end of his stay in early
May. Two days after his arrival, William personally called on
his guest, followed the next day by Prince George of Denmark,
husband of Anne, the future Queen of England. Peter returned
the king's visit at Kensington Palace; at the request of his host,
he consented to sit for the famous portrait painter, Sir Godfrey
Kneller.[137] Within a fortnight, according to Luttrell, "The Tsar
has been several times privately to wait on his Majesty at Kensington."[138]

Details of the red carpet treatment received by Peter during
his sojourn in England are well known. Suffice to note here that
in three-and-a-half months, the tsar had an opportunity not only
to study the principles underlying British shipbuilding at the
Deptford Royal Docks, but also inspected naval and military
arsenals and witnessed fleet maneuvers specially arranged for
him. He visited churches, museums, libraries, centers of learn-
ing,and exchanged ideas with distinguished Anglican church-
men, scholars, engineers, and influential persons of all walks of
life.[139] Although William issued a proclamattion in early February, "prohibiting his majesties subjects to enter into the service
of foreign princes and states without lycence,"[140] Peter was al-
lowed to hire some sixty specialists for service in Russia, many
of whom were recommended by Lord Carmarthen and Admiral
Mitchell, as was the case with Aberdeen University mathemati-
cian Henry Farquharson, founder of a School of Mathematics
and Navigation in Moscow.[141]

It is difficult to believe that all this was done only because
William "knew that his attempts to bring about peace between
Austria and Turkey would anger the Tsar and . . . he took pains
in other directions to please him."[142] To Peter, the manifold
gestures of British friendship seemed genuine and served as
proofs that the *entente cordiale* visualized by him at Utrecht
had solid foundations. Indeed for about six months such assumptions may not have been entirely unrealistic. It was only in

early January, 1698, that the first Turkish peace feelers reached London in the wake of the defeats suffered at the hand of the imperial forces in the preceding year, and it took two additional months before "the grand vizier had sent for the English and Dutch ambassadors to desire them to mediate a peace between the Turks and the emperor." It was the end of March when the secretary of British ambassador Lord Paget, "who came hither in 40 days from Constantinople, is gone back with letters to his excellency: 'tis certain that the grand seignior desires our kings mediation, to make peace between him and the emperor."[143]

While the nature and scope of the Turkish willingness to enter into peace negotiations with Vienna had to be ascertained, William recieved the alarming news that the death of the ailing and childless Charles II of Spain was imminent. Approached by Louis XIV to enter into a secret alliance with him so they could dictate their terms to the rest of Europe and avoid a war over the Spanish succession, the king was also pressed by Leopold I for support against France.[144] William doubted the good faith of the French, but he knew that as long as the emperor continued his war against the Turk, England and Holland could expect no effective help from Vienna and the burden of fighting another war against Louis would fall upon them. Groping toward the acceptance of the First Partition Treaty based on the offer of Louis XIV which he signed in August, William,[145] who was his own foreign secretary, nevertheless found himself on the horns of a dilemma. Consequently, he worked hard for a separate peace between Vienna and Constantinople to strengthen his hand vis-à-vis France in case of the Spanish king's death. But he kept his mediation secret from Peter, whom he wished to keep as an ally at least as long as the outcome of the mediation was uncertain, the troubles in Poland persisted and "the Richelieu system" securing French hegemony over the continent[146] might be revived. As a counterpoint to Peter who thought that the Peace of Ryswick would liberate imperial forces for a more vigorous pursuit of the war in the Orient and thus come to the aid of Muscovy, William hoped that peace with the Sublime Porte wold enable the emperor to contribute more effectively to the containment of France in the West. Although these two political concepts appear incompatible in retrospect, it was far from evident in the spring of 1698 which of them would ultimately prevail, because all the rulers of major powers held more than one iron in the fire at the same time.

VII

Erosion of the Anglo-Russian *Entente Cordiale*

There remains one final implication of the Anglo-Russian *entente cordiale,* namely, its place in the politics of east central Europe. While still in London, Peter heard with indignation of Turkish peace proposals. He did not refrain from indicating during his farewell visit to William at the end of April that he deemed them premature and that he resented being circumvented in the negotiations. Although the tsar was courteous and thanked the king for his hospitality, William subsequently sent his regrets and tried to explain the reasons for his secretiveness. But by that time, Peter was already in Vienna.[147]

Upon his return to Holland, the tsar learned more about the sultan's peace initiatives in Vienna and Venice transmitted by the British who anticipated the renewal of hostilities with Louis XIV over the Spanish succession. Through his representative in Warsaw, the tsar was invited by the emperor to send Russian envoys to participate in the negotiations with Constantinople.[148] In addition to the information given to him by the leaders of the Great Embassy who did not go with him to England, Peter was also warned by the ambassador of Augustus II that Leopold I was considering a separate peace with the Ottoman Empire. In his reply to the emperor's invitation to send a representative to the planned peace congress, the Polish king in fact indicated that before entering negotiations with the Turks, he first would like to have the opportunity to consult "with our ally the Grand Duke of Muscovy" (*cum Colligato Nostro Magno Moschorum Duce*) concerning points of mutual interest.[149]

First reluctant to give credence to the news concerning his Austrian ally's willingness to "break his word,"[150] the tsar hastened to Vienna, hoping to convince Leopold I of the merits of the Russian viewpoint. Although constrained by Habsburg etiquette and a measure of high-handedness by court officials who gave him to understand that imperial sovereignty was superior to that of other monarchs, the impetuous Peter surprised his hosts and foreign ambassadors by his civilized behavior.[151] Even though he ignored some of the ceremonial restrictions agreed upon before his fifteen-minute private audience with the emperor, the tsar's Russian address to his imperial "brother," rendered by General Lefort immediately into German, was most respectful: calling Leopold the greatest among Christian monarchs, Peter confirmed the alliance existing between their respective countries. Almost apologetically, he explained the delay in paying his respects to the aging emperor by referring to the urgency of equipping his naval forces in Holland and England, an argument which he was to use again in the political negotiations with Bohemian Chancellor Count Kinsky that followed. To the tsar's deferential attitude Leopold reacted graciously stressing Peter's services to the whole of Christianity.[152] Yet subsequent exchanges with Kinsky showed that beyond the diplomatic pleasantries, the Austrian and Russian approaches to the "Eastern Question" differed rather sharply.

In spite of his suspicions that the peace of Ryswick was not going to endure, the tsar hoped that the cessation of hostilities in the west would strengthen his alliance with the Empire and perhaps even lead to the Maritime Powers' financial and naval

Monsieur

La Porte étant présentement tout disposé à vouloir sincèrement la Paix, et sa Sac. Ma. Imp.le ayant (comme V. E. a eu la bonté de m'écrire) les mêmes inclinations, J'espère que les difficultés que pourroient suggérer ceux qui préfèrent l'interêt particulier, à celui du public, ne seront pas capable d'apporter de l'empêchement à l'accomplissement d'un si bon œuvre, Mais comme le Dessein de ceux qui ne désirent pas la paix va à retarder la negotiation, nôtre soin ne doit aller qu'à l'avancer, c'est pour cette Raison que Je prie V. E. de presser les choses vivement, pour prévenir aux accidens qui pourroient arriver à Détourner les bonnes dispositions, et à fin qu'ayant nos expéditions, nous puissions sans différer d'avantage, arrêter le fondement de la Paix sur l'Uti possidetis, pour, après agiter par Commissaires les autres Circonstances, (Limites, Démolition, ou échange de Places et autres points considérables) Pour solliciter cet expédition,

7. June 19, 1698 letter of Lord Paget, British Ambassador to Constantinople, to Bohemian Chancellor Count Kinsky, regarding the Porte's willingness to enter peace negotiations on the basis of *uti possidetis*. Courtesy Österreichisches Staatsarchiv, Vienna. Cf. p. 92, n. 153, below.

mon Secretaire fût renvoyé a Vienne le 10, du mois passé, et pour Mieux entretenir, et menager la Bonne disposition (en attendant son retour) (le Gr. Vizir l'ayant ainsi desiré) nous accompagnons son Altesse, a Belgrade, vers la quelle place nous avençons presentement etant aujourd'huy a deux journés près de Philipopoli; Je prens la liberté d'importuner V.E. dans l'Opinion que desirant la paix, elle agreéra le zele qui me porte a la faire rehisir, Depuis le depart de mon secretaire, J'ay reçu la lettre du 29 May que V.E. me fit l'honneur de m'ecrire pour accompagner la lettre de son E. Monsr Ruzini Ambr pour la Sereme Republ: De Venise a Vienne que V.E. a eu la bonté de me procurer, et dont il la remercié très humblement, Je supplie V.E. de lui faire tenir la reponse incluse, et de croire que ie suis avec un profond respect, et une parfaite sincerité

De V.E.

Cazali
o 19 Juin S.t 1698

Je supplie V.E. de faire tenir les incluses a la direction.

Le très Humble et le
très Obeissant serviteur

G. Paget

7. Paget's letter of June 19, 1698 continued.

Pagett

de dat. 19 Junÿ 698

P.ᵗ 22 Julÿ, von
peter gvamalein auß per
Stafettam geschickt

P.ᵗ 16 dito rc.

7. Paget's letter of June 19, 1698 continued.

Copia

Plenipotentiæ pro me C.
Khinsky ad subscribendam
declarationem Turcis in p^to
pacis faciendam dd 23 Junÿ

8. Copy of the Latin document (June 23, 1698) investing Count Kinsky
with full power to negotiate peace with Turkey on behalf of Leopold I and
his allies, Venice, Poland and Muscovy, via British mediation, on the basis
of *uti possidetis*. Courtesy Österreichisches Staatsarchiv, Vienna. Cf. pp.
55, 57-58, and 92, n. 149 below.

Leopoldus.

Notum testatumq facimus
tenore praesentium Universis
quod cum ad tractatus pacis
Nos inter, Nostrosq foederatos
ex una: Et excelsam Portam
Ottomanicam ex altera partibus
concilianda per Serenissmi
et potentissimi Magnae Britaniae
Regis, Ordinumq Generalium
foederati Belgii legatos,
mediationis causa in Turcia exis
"tentes, via patefacta sit, Nos
pro eo ad negotium tam salu
"tare Nostra ex parte promo"
"vere cupimus, Illustri et Ma"
"gnifico fideli Nobis dilecto
Francisco Udalrico Comiti Kinsky,
Consiliario Nostro intimo, et
Supremo Regni Nostri Bohemiae
Cancellario plenam et amplam
facultatem ac potestatem

8. Copy of Latin document of June 23, 1698 continued.

dedcrimus et concesserimus, pro
ut hisce animo bene-deliberato
damus et concedimus ad Subscri
bendum et Sigillo suo muniendum
Declarationem, cui et Inclytæ
Reipublicæ Venetæ in aula
Nostra legatus, ad hunc actum
speciali mandato constitutus
chirographum apposuit, et
sigillum suum impressit, quæq
dictis legatis Mediatorijs datur
potestas declarandi pro accepto
et Stabilito, Nostro, et prædictæ
Reipublicæ Venetæ nomine, cum
Iuris fundamenti Universalis
parti seu regulæ Uti possi
detis, Eiusdemq pro fœderatis
Nostris Siliceq Serenissimis
et potentissimis Rege, et Re
publica Polona, nec non
Czaro et magno Duce Moxo,
vix utiliter Stipulandæ, eo
fine et adjecta conditione, ut

Simul eôdemq passû similem
declarationem acceptabi fundâ
menti prædicti illis cossideratis
pro nobis, nostrisq fœderatis
Porta Ottomana, pro sua parte
faciat, et traditô pariter per
plenipotentia nos nos simili
Declarationis jnstrumentô, quam
„primùm locô destinatô ad„
Congressum procedatur, in quo
sub auspicijs receptæ media„
„tionis, eiusq legatorum offi„
„cijs mediatorijs per pleni„
„potentianos partium belli„
„gerantium sufficientibus man„
„datis ab utrinq instructos,„
de omnium et singulorum
fœderatorum rationibus
seû jnteresse, ut vocant,
agatur tracteturq; pro„
mittentes in Verbo nostro

8. Copy of Latin document of June 23, 1698 continued.

Imperatorio et Regio, quod,
quidquid declaratione istâ
per proeditum Plenipotentia"
rium Nostrum obsignatâ conti"
netur, id omne ratum firmumq
habere velimus, et debeamus.
Harum vigore literarum, manu
Nostrâ Subscriptarum, et sigilli
nostri Caesarei appressione mu"
nitarum, quae dabantur Viennae

8. Copy of Latin document of June 23, 1698 continued.

9. Copy of the May 31, 1698, Latin letter of the King of Poland, attached to the preceding document which appointed Kinsky to be the emperor's plenipotentiary at the peace negotiations with the Ottoman Porte. Augustus advised preliminary consultations with the Grand Duke of Muscovy, Peter. Courtesy Österreichisches Staatsarchiv, Vienna. Cf. pp. 54 and 92, n. 149, below.

conditiones. Magnum Oratorem
seu Comissarium expedituri sumus,
ubi primùm cum Colligato Nostro
Magno Moschorum Duce collata
uti interest, habuerimus consilia
opportunitàsqp, ipsa expediendi
supervenerit: Interim Extraordi-
narium Ablegatum ad Maj:tes
Vram designandum prope diem
mittemus, qui momentis rerum,
atqp huic negotio diligenter
attendat, ulterioresqp Illius
hac super re sensus Nobis re-
ferat. De coetero Majestatem
Vram inter continuos prosperi-
tatem successus optimè valere
animitus precamur. Dabantz
Varsaviæ die 31. May 1698.

Ihro Durchlaucht Wohlgeborne Herr,
sollte sich davon nicht mehr der
die übrige seiner besonderen
zu seiner grossen gestalte con-
fidentz, sondern auch, da der
König Maj: der Republieq vor
allem dann, was Ihro circa negotium pacis auss trustfry is-
zu,

9. Copy of King of Poland's letter of May 31, 1698 continued.

3 July 698

J'ay reçeu avec tout estime et
mils obligations, l'honneur de
la lettre de V.Ex.ᵃ du 9 May passé
portée par son Secretaire le
3ᵐᵉ du Juin passé la reponce
a été tardée par le concert
qu'il y a fallu prendr' entre l'Emp.
mon Seigneur et Maître et
la Republique de Venise, dont
l'Ambassad.ʳ residant á cette cour
n'a voulu y faire un pas sans
ordr' expres des ses maîtres, J'ay
fait rapport á l'Emp. de tout
ce, que V.E. m'avoit mandé, soit
par sa lettre commune avec
Mons.ʳ l'Ambassad.ʳ Coliers, soit
par sa particuliére, S.M.Imp.ᵉˡ
a reçeu le tout, avec sa bonté
estim.ᵉ et reconnoissance ordi,,
,,naire, Sachant bon gré aux
fattigués qu'Elle se donne pour
mener á bon port ce salutair'
ouvrage et en conservera tou,,
,,jours une memoire reconnoissante
J'avois creu, que par ma lettre
ostensible du 24 Avril passé

10. Count Kinsky's July 3, 1698, letter to Ambassador Paget. While accepting the principle of *uti possidetis* on behalf of the emperor and Venice,
Kinsky indicates the Polish vacillations concerning the peace congress and
the presence of the tsar in Vienna for the last 6-7 days promising further
information of the negotiations with the latter. Courtesy Österreichisches
Staatsarchiv, Vienna. Cf. p. 93, n. 153 below.

avoir donné en main de V.E. tout
ce qu'il fallu pour arrester sous
les conditions y exprimées la reigle
de l'Uti possidetis pour l'Emp:
et la Republique de Venise, si les
Turcs y fussent venü aussi de leur
part, et je suis chagriné de ce, que
je m'y suis trompé, ainsi que je
l'ay veu par sa dite lettre, mais
comm'il ne s'agit, que d'asseurer
les Turcs de cette reigle de l'uti
possidetis de nôtre part aussi
si Eux y viennent à même tems
et sous les conditions portées par
ma lettre ostensible, ainsi nous
croyons avoir amplement
suppléés à tout le defaut par
l'instrument de nôtre Declaration
que nous envoyons cy joint
Suppliant Vos EE: comme me,
"diateurs d'en faire l'usage, qu'
elles jugeront devoir faites au
cas que les Turcs viennent d'ac,
"repter la même reigle pour
Euxe sous les conditions y por,
"tées, sans l'accomplissements
des quelles l'Emp:r ne sçauroit
avec la Republique de Venise
sauf la bonne foy des alliances

la tenir pour acceptée de leur
part, me rapportant, quant
à cela au contenü de nôtre
Sudite declaration, et à la lettre
commune que je me donne l'hon
neur d'écrir à vos EE.ces comm
Ambassad.rs Mediateurs reçeus
de part, et d'autres, nous ne
Saurions l'accepter, que pour
l'Emp.r et la Republique de
Venise, car pour ce, qu'est
de la Pologne, V.E. verra de
la cy jointe coppie de la
lettre de ce Roy à l'Emp.r qu'il
ne s'oppose pas au congrès
mais aussi ne se declar il pas
Sur l'acceptation, ou rejet de
l'Utipossidetis. Pour ce
qu'est du G.d Car de Moscovie
maintenant present icy depuis
6 ou 7 jours nous en traiton.
avec luy, et j'auray l'honneu
d'aviser à V.E. du Succès de
ce negoce en peu de jours
cependant si les Turs se decla
rent à l'acceptation de cet
uti possidetis sous les condition
proposées par l'Emp.r, et que

10. Copy of Count Kinsky's letter of July 3, 1698 continued.

la dessus l'Emp.r et Venise n'étans
pas d'avis de remetre ce point
essentiel á un traitté de Commissai
re reciproquement aprés la paix
faite deputés pour ce negoce,
mais desirants pour des bonnes
raisons, que tout cela soit en gros
et en detaill defini, arrêté, et con
clü dans ce congrés en égard
de quoy l'on a mis dans la com
mune declaration, qu'en ce
congrés il faut traitter et con
venir de ce, que pour faciliter
la paix on pourroit faire per
evacuationem, demolitionem,
vel etiam permutationem, pp.

Or quans au têms de venir
á ce congrés V.E. trouverà que
sous la condicion d'y venir im
mediatement aprés que la regle
de l'uti possidetis serà recipro
quement entre l'Emp.r, la Re
publique de Venise et la Porte
Ottomanne sous les condicions
portées recue et établie, ne
convenans pas á l'Emp.r et
á Venise, d'y vivre aprés cela
long têms in incerto, mais

10. Copy of Count Kinsky's letter of July 3, 1698 continued.

d'en sortir promptement soit par la paix faic, ou par la continuation de la guerre. Si que V.E. serà servie de penetrer là dessus les sentiments des Turcs, et de nous en aviser promptement. Pour le lieu et la maniere du congrés V.E. trouverà que j'en parle fort amplement dans ma lettre pour eux deux commune, j'ajouteray seulement, qu'il y a mils raisons qui devroient obliger les Turcs à n'y pas refuser Vienne, veu que cette fameuse Trenve, de l'an 1606, 1620, es tous le reste de paix faites pendans ce siecle y ont étées conclues, es tous jours traitées sur le territoire des Empereurs Romains, si toute fois les Turcs le vouloient y roidir et ne s'y rendr' à la raison, on leur offre Debresin lieu le plus commode, qu'on aye pù trouver pour cela. Il seroit inutile de parler d'un Armistice à faire pendans cette Campagne, ou le Congrés, car l'Emp. et Venise n'y s'auroient

10. Copy of Count Kinsky's letter of July 3, 1698 continued.

venir soit par la raison de leur
jnterêt, soit par les oppositions
que la Pologne, et la Moscovie
y pourroient faire sur le fondement
des alliances contractées avec les
susdites puissances. Voicy Mr.
re, que J'ay pû dir à V.E. sur le
negoce, qui roule pour le bon
succés du quel souhaitans á
elle mille bonheurs, J'auray
l'honneur d'être et demeurer
et par obligation, et par re,,
connoissance p

ps.
Me donnant l'honneur de par
,,ter à V.E. comme je fais, je crois
l'insinuer assés clairement
çe qu'est de l'état de nôtre
Campagne à l'égard de la
quelle je ne veux paroître
ny fanfaron, ny detracteur

Monsieur

Par le rtour de mon secretaire (y $\frac{5}{15}$ courant
j'ay veu, aude le rspet que je dois et avec une
entiere reconoissance, la lettre du 3me Juillet que V.
E. me fit l'honneur de m'escrire, et Je me riouis
extremement, de conoitre par là, que Sa Sacré Maté,
Impble agréé Benignement les Offices qui ont été em-
ploiés, par ses Ordres, pour son service, et que les
soins et les applications, dont on s'est servi, ont
mis la Negotiation de Paix en un si bon etat qu'il
y'a Esperance qu' Elle puisse terminer à la satisfaction des Puissances interessées,
Je demande Excuse à V, E, si Je n'ay pas pû comprendre
par la lettre du, 24, d'Avril passé, que nous aurions
toute Authorité necessaire pour arreter le fondement
d'Uti possidetis; etant dit là dedans Citatis et expres-
curioribus Serenissimo Regi et Reipublica Polona facta
est propositionis Ottomanica communicatio, a quibus
responsa, ubi primum appulerint, E∮ sine mora pro
depressum communicata, transmittentur &c; et plus

125

11. Paget's reply of July 24, 1698, to Kinsky's letter of July 3 insists that
the principle of *uti possidetis* must apply to the peace treaties with Poland
and Muscovy as well lest the Turks take advantage of the disunity of the
Allies. Courtesy of Österreichisches Staatsarchiv, Vienna. Cf. p. 93, n. 153
and 154.

et plus avant, Reliquum adhuc est, Pacis fanciendæ obstaculum, ex eo Natum, quod altissime memoratæ Sa. Cæ. et Regiæ Majis. præcactisqs suis Serenissimis Fœderatis commune sit cum Magno Moscoviæ Tzaro Fœdus, cuius, cum nulla sit in Ottomanica Propositione facta mentio &c.

Par la dernière du 3.me Juillet que V.E. eut la Bonté de m'adresser ces difficultés sont expliqués en declarant que l'Uti Possidetis, étant posé pour fondement de traité pour sa Sa. Maje. Imple. et Ses Alliés; si le Roy de Pologne, et le Tzar de Moscovie n'agréent pas l'Offre, Sa Mad. Imple. et la Serenissime Repe. de Venize consentent, néanmoins, à la Paix, à la quelle puis après les autres seront Obligés d'entrer; Cette particularité pourtant quoi qu'expliqué dans la Déclaration de Vos E. ... n'est pas, ce me semble, bien compris par la Porte, qui Croit que l'Uti Possidetis, est aussi bien établi pour fondement de Paix pour la Pologne et la Moscovie, comme pour sa Maje. Impl., et la Repub. de Venize, et que ce qui est couché dans la Declaration n'est que touchant le tems de Conference avec ces Ministres, qu'on diffère à Cause de la distance des lieux, &c.; Cependant, puisque là dessus ils n'ont point fait aucune difficulté, ni demandé aucune explication, je ne me crûs pas obligé, d'en parler aucunement, pour ne pas les effaroucher avec des difficultés qui ne sont pas, essentielles, étant que Ces Puissances, se trouveront, on Obligés à s'y Conformer, ou bien, à prendre des Mesures qui ne sçauroient être qu' avantageuses à la Porte, ce qu' indubitablement ils ne feront pas; L' Uti Possidetis, étant donc accepté sur les conditions portés par la Declaration de Sa Majé. Impe. et de la Repub. de Venise, comme apparoît par les papiers presentement envoyés à V. E.; dans les quelles (quoi qu'on ne se soit pas servi des mêmes paroles, ayant voulu suivre, en leur Declaration, le stile et manière du Pais) ils veulent, et entendent la même chose; et ainsi ont ils declaré; me semble qu'on devroit commencer les Conferences, à quoi de ce coté icy on s'est déjà preparé, come elle pourra voir par la lettre Commune; On a essayé par tous les Detours, dont on se peut aviser, d'induire ces Messieurs à vouloir passer à Vienne pour traiter; Mais ils ont d'abord declaré resolument, qu'ils ne vouloint pas traiter que dans une place Neutre, ny passer les frontières en aucune manière; Pour lieu de Traité, ils ont Proposé Salankemen, ou aucune place plus commode, dans ces Environs; Cela etant, il faudra que les Mediateurs soient Campés, et restent dans leurs Tentes, où, l'on sera, sujet aux incommodités de L'Air, du froid, des pluyes, neiges, et du mauvaise tems; Mais en esperance, que, les fondemens etant posés, les Circonstances ne pourront pas nous detenir long tems, On se soumettra Volontiers aux accidans, pour faciliter la conduite, et la

126

Paget
de dat 24 July 698

conclusion d'un si grand Bien, De V.E. (qui a parfaite
connoissance de ces choses) Je supplie être informé que
formalités on doit observer au Congrès; On a parlé
ces jours passés d'un Armistice, disant, que, puisque le
fondement de la Paix est arrêté en substance (quoy que
touttes les formalités n'y soyent point passées) Et que par
les accidans de la Campagne, il pourroit arriver du
changement aux affaires, qui altereroient la Negotiation
il seroit necessaire d'y penser; Mais, leur ayant dit que
cela ne se pouvoit accorder, mais qu'au contraire on
avoit declaré ne vouloir aucunement consentir à cela
ils ne l'ont pas pressé davantage; Je ne m'étends pas
sur ces particularités, parceque de tout, elle sera
plainement informé, par le present Envoyé; Et Je
ne veux pas l'incommoder inutilement; Je supplie
V.E. de me presenter aux pieds de sa Maj.té Imp.le Et
de l'assurer de la sincerité Et continuation de mes
tres humbles devoirs; Je prie, aussi, V.E. de croire
que Je suis, avec un tres profond respect, Et avec
une parfaite sincerité, de V.E.

July 14/24 dans le Camp
Ottoman, auprès Sofia
1698.

Le tres humble, tres Obligé,
Et tres Obeissant serviteur

G. Paget

11. Paget's reply of July 24, 1698 continued.

aid in the anti-Turkish war. None of these hopes materialized and Peter's most bitter disappointment was caused by Austria. Having won a major military victory over the Turks at Zenta in Southern Hungary under the command of Prince Eugene of Savoy ten days after Peter's meeting with William at Utrecht, the imperial forces expelled Ottoman power from almost the entire territory of Hungary. This enabled Leopold to accept the Turkish offer to start peace negotiations on the principle of *uti possidetis,* by keeping the territories conquered in the course of the war. But the Russian desire to acquire Kerch, which controlled the exist from Azov to the Black Sea, could not be based on that principle; yet without achieving this goal, the *raison d'être* of Peter's enormous investment in his naval program would be wasted.

In vain did the tsar insist that he was entitled to be consulted by his ally before the latter's acceptance of the general principles of the negotiations proposed by the Turks: he was presented with a *fait accompli* by the Austrians, who had agreed to the Turkish proposals on behalf of their Venetian, Polish and Russian allies, antedating documents in fact signed only after the Great Embassy's arrival in Vienna.[153] Peter pointedly noted in his interview with Kinsky that the emperor's wish to conclude peace with the sultan was motivated by the anticipated War of Spanish Succession, which did not justify the abandonment of his Russian ally; further, that the unrest which erupted in Hungary in the previous year might flare up again if imperial troops were to be transferred from that country to the French front, a prediction which proved prophetic in five years. But in July, 1698, the tsar's efforts resulted only in a guarded Austrian promise to support the Russian claims at the forthcoming peace negotiations with the Sublime Porte.[154] Although Peter found himself forced to reach an agreement with the Turks in Constantinople in 1700 following the Austrian-Turkish peace concluded at Carlowitz, the diplomatic cooperation motivated by the Ottoman danger, which began between Austria and Muscovy in the late fifteenth century and was reinforced by a series of treaties (1684, 1689, and 1697) during Peter's reign in the wake of the Turkish siege of Vienna in 1683, came to a turning point as a result of the negative impressions evoked in Peter by the Viennese political atmosphere.

Disillusionment with Austria contributed importantly to the tsar's decision to find an alternative to Russia's plans in the Black Sea region, the single-handed implementation of which was beyond her strength at that juncture of history.[155] Whether it was Augustus the Strong of Saxony and Poland, who first articulated the idea of a military alliance against Sweden or whether the suggestion came from the tsar at their Rawa Ruska meeting on the occasion of the latter's return from Vienna to Moscow, the "Swedish Question" loomed large on the Russian mind, and not only because of the alleged inadequate reception of the Great Embassy in Riga at the beginning of its *grand tour* used subsequently as a pretext by Peter himself.[156] A Russian drive to the Baltic had been tried by other Muscovite rulers, including Ivan the Terrible, and had a certain historical justification. It received open encouragement during the Great Embassy's negotiations with Brandenburg and found a veiled expression in Peter's Utrecht address to William III. Given Muscovy's geographic situation and her tsar's determination to make Russia a maritime power, the only alternative to the push to the Black Sea in the southeast was one toward the northwest in the Baltic area. Resentment caused by what seemed the betrayal of his most important ally, Leopold I, made Peter more receptive to the idea of war against Sweden.

Russian dissatisfaction was not confined to Austria. When the terms of the treaty of Carlowitz, concluded with the Porte by the Holy Roman Empire, Venice and Poland in January, 1699, failed to meet Peter's exaggerated demands, Ambassador Prokopii B. Voznitsyn, the tsar's representative at the peace congress, signed only a two-year truce with the Turks. But the ambassador, who was the third-ranking official leader of the

Great Embassy, advised his sovereign to initiate direct negotiations with Constantinople. Following this advice, Peter appointed another experienced diplomat, Emelian I. Ukraintsev, as special ambassador to the sultan,[157] requesting at the same time the mediation of William III in Constantinople.

In a letter to his "Most Serene Lord, Brother, and most affectionated Friend," written less than two years after they first met in Utrecht,[158] the tsar referred to "the peace agreed upon between his Imperiall Majestie of Germany, and other Potentates, through the mediation of Your Royall Majestie's ambassadors . . . at Sirmy off Carlowitz with the Turkish Court" indicating also why "Our Czar's Majestie's ambassador in the years of peace could not attain to have that satisfaction which others have gotten" on the foundation of "uti possidetis." "Forced not to stand off from the others" the ambassador agreed to a cessation of arms for two years. Yet desirous "to come to a full agreement. . . . Wee—the Great Lord Our Czar's Majesty have now sent to the Turkish Sultan Our extraordinary envoy" and

> desire friendly Our loving Brother the Great Lord his Royall Majestie will be pleased to order Your Royall Majestie's ambassador now residing by the Turkish Sultan in Constantinople, that he as a friend and mediator should be assistant to Our extraordinary envoy in all his agreements, that he may obtain that which other confederates have gotten, viz.: either longer time of cessation of arms, or an everlasting peace on Our side.

In ironic contrast to this flowery request for British mediation in Constantinople is the letter's opening reminder which reads like a reproach to the tsar's erstwhile hero:

> While Wee were with Your Royall Majestie for a certain time past *in the year 1698 it was not make knowne to Us concerning the mediation of Your Royall Majestie* between the confederates of his Imperiall Majestie of Germany, and other Christian Potentates, and the Turk; although Wee the Great Lord Our Czars Majestie, have

been helpful in these sacred warrs above others, with God Almighty's
assistance, in confounding the armys of the unbelievers, assisting his
Imperiall Majestie of Germany, and with him have had for certain
years a defensive and offensive allyance, and still have the same as it
is well knowne to the Great Lord Your Royall Majestie . . . [159]

The July 1699 letter to William III was in sharp contrast with
the tsar's Utrecht speech. It marked the end of Peter's crusading
mood, just like the Treaty of Carlowitz "ended the last war
which had at least begun, with the Holy League of 1684, as a
crusade."[160] It coincided with the arrival of a most important
Swedish official embassy in Moscow at a time when secret negotiations for an offensive anti-Swedish Danish-Saxon-Russian
alliance had all but been completed and Peter needed a peace
settlement with the Turks to have a free hand in the Baltic.[161]
Consequently, his previous preoccupation with the idea of an
anti-Turkish Holy War underwent a change, too. Six months
before the *cri de coeur* voiced in the tsar's letter to William,
Voznitsyn, who had been permanently accredited to the imperial court at the time of the Great Embassy's sojourn in Vienna,
was contacted by a French secret agent. Three weeks after Carlowitz, the agent expressed the opinion to the Russian ambassador
that Peter would be welcome in France. Eight days later the
French envoy, notified by Voznitsyn along with other members
of the diplomatic corps about his arrival in Vienna, called on
his Muscovite colleague and the Russian ambassador returned
the official visit within a week. In the course of their friendly
exchanges, faithfully reported to Moscow, the two diplomats
agreed that the world would benefit from the cooperation of
their respective sovereigns. Voznitsyn's discussions with the
Marquis de Villars, a future Marshal of France who was to play
an important role in the Spanish War of Succession, touched
on a variety of topics including Prince Lichtenstein's insulting
attitude toward the French representative, the Turks' fear of
the tsar, a Christian Monarch's duty to fight the infidels rather

than fellow-Christians, the advantages of French trade with Archangel, the respective ages of their sovereigns and Louis XIV's dynastic claims to the Spanish crown.[162] Although the Viennese encounters of the French and Russian representatives do not seem to have led to any practical consequences, the fact that they took place at all was significant in view of the total absence of Franco-Russian contacts in Holland at the time of the Ryswick peace negotiations. The conduct of Petrine diplomacy grew more complicated and signals were being changed in Moscow after the disappointment of Carlowitz.

To be sure, Russia's status as a permanent and important factor in the European state system began to be recognized, particularly by France, only after Peter's victory over the Swedes at Poltava in 1709, even though Franco-Russian diplomatic soundings had continued intermittently, on occasion with the tsar's personal participation, since 1701. Despite Peter's frequent travels abroad, his overdue journey to France materialized only in 1717. In part as a result of the deterioration of Russo-British relations, subsequent years witnessed a series of negotiations between the Russian and French courts aimed at entering into a political and dynastic alliance neither of which, however, proved to be feasible.[163]

Still, in one area at least, Louis XIV and Peter I acted along parallel lines in the early years of the Spanish War of Succession and the Great Northern War. The outbreak of new hostilities with France resulted in a weakening of Austrian occupational forces in Hungary, and this helped, as the tsar had predicted, the anti-Habsburg uprising that began in 1703 under the leadership of the Transylvanian Prince Francis II Rákóczi one year after Leopold's declaration of war on Louis XIV. The king of France regarded the Hungarian rebellion as a useful diversion, giving Rákóczi financial assistance, sending him a number of French officers as military advisors, intervening in his behalf in Poland and instructing his envoy in Constantinople to request

Turkish aid for Hungary; but Louis XIV refrained from entering
into a formal agreement with Rákóczi and from thus fully ex-
ploiting the opportunity to weaken the Habsburgs.[164]

Following his French colleagues example as early as 1704,
Peter's representatives at the Sublime Porte also bribed Ottoman officials with the double purpose of engaging the Turks in
the Western rather than the Northern war and of exerting pressure on the emperor to ponder the tsar's offer to help him with
Russian troops against the Hungarians. But when Augustus II
was defeated and forced by the Swedes to abdicate his Polish
crown in 1706, Peter initiated direct negotiations with Rákóczi
considering him as an alternative to Stanislas Leszczynski,
Sweden's candidate for the Polish throne. In view of the Hungarian leader's popularity among segments of the Polish nobility
and good connections with Paris, Peter's ambiguous diplomacy
was also motivated by the endeavor to obtain French mediation
to settle his conflict with Charles XII. This is clear from the
Hungarian-Russian negotiations and the cautiously worded text
of the treaty concluded in Warsaw in September, 1707, and duly
signed by Rákóczi in October and Peter in December of the
same year.[165]

The treaty, which refers to Rákóczi as a "Prince of the Holy
Roman Empire and Transylvania and Leader of Confederated
Hungary," obliged Rákóczi to accept the crown of Poland if
freely elected by the Polish estates and the tsar to support him
with all his might and military forces. It also stipulated the observation of a 3-4 months waiting period in the course of which
a Franco-Bavarian mediation was to be attempted to establish
peace with Sweden. In case of a Swedish attack on Hungary, the
tsar offered his military and financial aid. He also promised to
do his utmost to prevail over the emperor to restore the freedom of Hungary and Transylvania, and to confirm Rákóczi as
prince of Transylvania. In case of a continued occupation of
Poland by Sweden, the tsar and the prince would enter into a

military alliance with each other. They also agreed to exchange residents.[166]

The rapidly changing military and international situation did not permit the implementation of the main provisions of the Russo-Hungarian alliance of 1707. At the time of its conclusion, Louis XIV had already been put on the defensive in Western Europe and his assistance to Rákóczi diminished considerably. Prior to the battle of Poltava, Charles XII controlled events in Poland, while after his defeat at the hands of Peter in 1709, the personal union between Saxony and Poland was restored under Augustus. The renewal of hostilities with Turkey in the following year made it impossible for the tsar to challenge Vienna openly in the midst of his struggle against the Swedish-Turkish alliance: his attempt to mediate between the emperor and Rákóczi was rejected by both, as had been earlier efforts of the Maritime Powers which feared the weakening of the Habsburgs. By 1711, Rákóczi's struggle was subdued by reinforced imperial power.[167]

The Warsaw Treaty of 1707 is nevertheless of considerable historical interest. It documents how Peter and Rákóczi wanted to break through that diplomatic isolation which threatened both the Hungarian and Russian struggles against enemies who seemingly belonged to two different warring camps but potentially threatened them both. When French help was no longer available, Rákóczi obtained the tsar's political support. Through his alliance with Rákóczi, Peter came very close to transforming the two simultaneously ongoing wars, the one over the Spanish succession and the other fought over the Baltic area, into one single global conflict. It was in the interest of the Grand Alliance including the Holy Roman Empire and the Maritime Powers to keep the two wars separate:[168] their estrangement from Russia and Peter's contemplation of French mediation in his conflict with Sweden and possibly of an alliance with Louis XIV, had the opportunity been seized upon by the latter three years earlier, could have changed the history of the world. Even though futile in many respects, the tsar's treaty with Rákóczi, signed on the tenth anniversary of his first meeting with William III at Utrecht, meant a reversal of some of Peter's most genuinely felt ideas about Russia's role and her chief partners with which he approached the sphere of international relations when he first thrust himself onto the European scene in 1697.

VIII

Summary and Afterthought

In concluding this *pièce à discussion,* it is argued on grounds of textual criticism and other historical evidence that the handwritten Utrecht speech of the "Muscovy Czar" in the Scottish National Library is both authentic and important. The English language manuscript strengthens, supplements and in a certain respect supersedes the evidence provided by Leo Loewenson over twenty-five years ago and used by Reinhard Wittram in his biography of Peter I and by Henri and Barbara van der Zee in their study of William and Mary.

Although no contemporary Dutch version of the tsar's speech has been found in archival sources so far[169] and the letters written to Grand Pensionary Antonius Heinsius by Amsterdam Burgomaster Nicolaas Witsen, who is said to have attended the Utrecht meeting between William and Peter do not mention an address by the latter,[170] the possibility of a Dutch primary text cannot be entirely excluded, as shown by the recent identification of what seems to be the first full-length contemporary handwritten English version of Peter's speech discovered at Edinburgh. It there were no handwritten Dutch version of the tsar's

63

Utrecht speech originally, then the Edinburgh manuscript may
have been copied from an English summary of notes taken by a
Dutch-speaking English participant in the meeting or a draft
prepared by or upon the order of an eyewitness, possibly William III himself, shortly after the meeting.

Such an interpretation by no means contradicts Luttrell's
pertinent reference according to which William "came to a pub-
lick house in Utrecht" where he first exchanged greetings with

> the three ambassadors of Muscovy . . . who made speeches by their
> interpreter full of complements and assurances of the great esteem
> and respect the czar had for his majesties person; and when they had
> received the kings answer, told him their master was come in person
> to confirm all they had said, and to entertain his majestie with mat-
> ters of great moment, praying his majestie would see him without
> much company: the king thereupon, with the duke of St. Albans,
> the earl of Westmorland, lord Villiers, earl of Albermarle, &c. went
> into the czars room, and having embrac'd each other, conferred to-
> gether by an interpreter 2 hours; . . .[171]

It will be noted that when Luttrell describes the first encounter between Peter and William under the date of September 7,
1697, he does not give "An abstract of the czars speech to his
majestie" which follows later, in an entry of October 14.[172] The
protocol part of the description mentions speeches made by the
Russian ambassadors and the king's answer and the ceremonial
was apparently translated by the interpreter of the Muscovite
delegation: but neither the ambassadors' greetings nor the king's
reply appear to have been preserved. The personal encounter
with the tsar seems to have been attended by several English
dignitaries in addition to the ambassadors and, possibly, by Amsterdam Burgomaster Witsen, was also assisted by an interpreter.
But the account does not identify the interpreter or the language
of translation in either of these two interlocking but separate
instances: whereas French may have been used on the first ceremonial occasion (as has been claimed) which, however, the tsar

did not attend, Peter may have resorted to Dutch in which he could freely express himself on the second, more intimate occasion. It may be observed here that among the persons mentioned by Luttrell on the British-Dutch side, the earl of Albemarle, Arnout Jouse van Keppel, was a Dutchman and William's favorite at the time. In view of Albemarle's key role in reading and drafting the king's confidential correspondence,[173] he was not only in a position of translating for his English peers what may have passed between Peter and William in Dutch at the meeting itself, but also may have prepared or ordered an English summary of Peter's speech, and its dissemination among the confidants of the court, or even its printing in French to strengthen the Grand Alliance in the ongoing war of nerves by giving the impression of an imminent Anglo-Russian *entente.*

The hypothesis just advanced may be corroborated by a hitherto unpublished French manuscript committed to paper about 1730 perhaps by Louis Lefort, secretary of the Muscovite Embassy, concerning the "History and Life of the General and Admiral Lefort." In these memoirs, an interesting passage on the tsar's encounter with King William at Utrecht goes in some respects beyond the information registered by Luttrell. This account identifies General Lefort as the Russian ambassadors' spokesman in their initial meeting with the king and claims that after accepting the invitation to visit with Peter in an adjacent room, William "went there with eight persons." In addition to stressing the cordial atmosphere of the meeting between the two princes, the report also mentions two of the topics on which their conversation focused, namely, the affairs of Poland and the peace negotiations at Ryswick. According to this account, "the king was very satisfied and very pleased with this conference which was sufficiently long and at which General Lefort served as the only interpreter. . . ."[174] But although the older Lefort may have been the interpreter provided for the occasion by the Russian side, the eight persons in

William's entourage must have included several who knew both French and Dutch in addition to English. Only further research may decide, who might have prepared the first summary of the tsar's address in English, Dutch, or perhaps French.[175] The circumstance that in addition to several English summaries we have two identical contemporary versions of the speech, one in English and one in French, and also that both have been preserved in Britain, demonstrates the significance attributed by at least some of William's confidants to the improvement of Anglo-Muscovite relations, especially in the field of commerce. The absence of any reference to Peter's address in the Russian records may be explained by the preeminence given in it to William and by its primary destination for foreign consumption at a time when the Muscovite public's knowledge about foreign affairs was minimal. But whether formulated by Lefort and conveyed in the tsar's presence or improvised by Peter, there can be no doubt that the Utrecht address expressed the latter's wish to give the impression that Russia was ready to expand her trade relations with the Maritime Powers, and to enter the anti-French coalition and play an active role in world affairs provided that she could get financial help for the pursuit of her war in the Orient and technological assistance for the modernization of her military establishment. While subsequent negotiations of the Great Embassy failed to obtain the financial subsidies desired, the tsar's efforts to recruit military-technical personnel and transfer western technology to Muscovy met with undeniable success.

Additional inquiry will also be required to determine how a copy of the tsar's address found its way into the Sutherland archives. The handwritten single page English text at Edinburgh is not attached to any other document and does not include any explanatory note or annotation. But we do have a few leads. A former émigré, George Gordon, the fourteenth earl of Sutherland, had been a most consistent supporter of William and Mary, and was appointed to the Privy Council of Scotland in May 1689. He was also present in six of the seven sessions of Parliament between 1689 and 1700, and his wife, Lady Jean Wemyss, was a close friend of Queen Mary.[176] Their son, John Lord Strathnaver, who became the fifteenth earl of Sutherland upon his father's death in 1703, was an active adherent of the Revolution of 1688 and played an important role in securing Scotland for William III. After 1692, he raised and commanded a regiment for several years in Flanders. In fact, a letter preserved in the family correspondence reveals that Lord Strathnaver was in Ghet in October, 1697, and was in touch with some influential person in the immediate circle of William at Loo regarding the proceedings of a court-martial related to a mutiny in his regiment.[177] Given Lord Strathnaver's physical proximity to Utrecht and his, and his father's, distinguished position, it is as good an explanation as any that he may have received one of the copies of the tsar's address circulated around the royal court shortly after the first meeting between William and Peter.

Turning to the significance of the tsar's Utrecht address, several points are salient. The unexpected, apparently sincere, and forceful formulation of Peter's notion of foreign policy with one stroke completed the break with the traditions of Muscovite diplomacy implied in the tsar's "incognito" trip to the West and marked the dramatic beginning of personal "summit" diplomacy later fully developed by Catherine II and Alexander I and practiced through the nineteenth century.

Given at a moment when "Russia was only just embarking on her new role as a permanent element in the European state system,"[178] the speech nevertheless revealed a combination of political, military and even economic ambitions, with global implications. Although beyond the Muscovite state's strength at the time of their articulation, these imperial ambitions represented a perhaps premature but nonetheless remarkable readiness to challenge the French system of security in both East Central and Western Europe.

This Faustian, ultimately frustrated vision for which Russia was as yet unprepared, is of undeniable biographic interest because it helps us understand the tsar's inner development through gradual disillusionment with his most appreciated allies in the critical years 1697-98. Peter's disillusionment may have reinforced those negative traits in his personality which manifested themselves in the cruel revenge on the *streltsi* upon his return from Europe and in the deviously treacherous manner in which he prepared his attack on Sweden.[179]

If his Utrecht address contains elements of spontaneous and romantic perceptions inspired by the long awaited personal encounter with William, the treaty with Rákóczi negotiated and drafted very carefully on his behalf by such experienced hands as Chancellor Count Gavriil I. Golovkin, Ambassador Prince Gregorii F. Dolgorukii and Director of Foreign Affairs Baron Peter F. Shafirov reflected Russian *Realpolitik* as approved by a seasoned autocrat. At the time of his first meeting with William, Louis XIV seemed to be the "Public Enemy" of Christian civilization in the eyes of the twenty-five year old ardent supporter of the anti-Turkish Holy League, who aspired to become England's sword against the "Christian Turk" like Maximilian of Bavaria. Yet the reference to French-Bavarian mediation during the war with Sweden in the treaty with Rákóczi ten years later placed a different emphasis on the same protagonists: this time, the Elector of Bavaria was the ally of Louis XIV to whom Rákóczi offered the Hungarian crown,[180] and Peter did not have any real qualms about changing alliances either. Ironically, the stillborn alliance with Rákóczi dictated by what seemed to be Russian *raison d'état* at that particular moment endured no longer than the romantic ideas expressed by the tsar at Utrecht.

Actually, the initiative taken by the tsar at Utrecht was no mere illusion and should not be taken lightly. Although history's first anti-French Anglo-Russian *entente* cannot be compared in endurance or effectiveness to the two countries' alliance during the anti-Napoleonic campaigns a century later, the simultaneity of Anglo-Dutch naval maneuvers with Muscovite troop movements in the fall of 1697, both of which were aimed at frustrating the projection of French military power into Poland and the Baltic, cannot be attributed to chance alone. Nor should we underestimate the cordiality and vigor with which the experienced William responded to the trusting approach of his much younger fellow-monarch for whom all doors opened in England upon his order. Reexamination of contemporary British sources proved that the king's attitude was also motivated by the demands for trade, especially tobacco diplomacy. According to the British documentary evidence, these topics were surely on the agenda of the two monarchs' first two-hour long personal discussion, in addition to Polish affairs and European peace.

Macauley's oft quoted dictum that the tsar's journey was "an epoch in the history, not only of his country but of our's, and of the world's," is still valid, as pointed out by Loewenson. According to Wittram, Peter's three-and-a-half months long visit to England was in a certain respect the high point of the journey.[181] It is less well known that the tsar's stay in England coincided with a British political crisis in the course of which Parliament refused a royal request for a standing army justified by expected new international complications, and even forced the dismissal of the king's Dutch guards. William, who considered "withdrawing from England,"[182] may have been more appreciative of a Russian ally on the continent than generally assumed.

To be sure, Bishop Burnet's emphasis on Peter's anticipated interest in the civilian-political-religious aspects of his visit to England was misplaced.[183] The tsar knew that Parliament was not invented for Muscovy and if he departed England "possessed with truer Notions of Government,"[184] his subsequent actions failed to show it. But whatever England's most distinguished churchman of the age of the Glorious Revolution may have written about Peter to his friends or in his posthumously published *History of His Own Time* after their frequent and lengthy discussions in early 1698, his later and more skeptical opinion must be taken with a grain of salt. As Professor Cracraft has suggested, the tsar may not have been inclined to promote the tenets of Protestantism in Russia, but the idea of monarchical supremacy over the church, explained to him by Burnet, was to be introduced into the realm of "the mighty Northern Emperour" subsequently "with far-reaching, indeed revolutionary consequences."[185] Even in his administrative and judicial reforms, where Peter followed primarily Swedish prototypes,[186] there are instances of occasional British influence as seems to have been the case with changes in the law of inheritance. The tsar's appreciation of British education has also been pointed out recently.[187]

Perhaps the most important and immediate practical result of the Anglo-Russian *entente cordiale* was the transfer of applied technology and technical personnel to Muscovy; the tsar received the far-reaching cooperation of his British hosts, who were fully aware of the fact that this technological assistance was to be used primarly for military purposes in the Orient or wherever else their impetuous guest elected to apply it.[188] The stimulus given by Peter's visit to England in the growth of economic and scientific links with Muscovy lasted for generations to come: the volume of Russo-British trade trebled between 1698 and 1708 and continued to increase through the eighteenth century.[189] The same holds true for the transmission of mathematical knowledge and the natural sciences.[190] These contacts outlasted the Anglo-Russian *entente* established at Utrecht, which, however, served as the original political framework for them. In this sense, the political role of science in Russia, stressed by Alexander Vucinich,[191] may be interpreted on interlocking historico-inspirational and military-utilitarian grounds as well.

Initiated by Peter and warmly encouraged by William, the first Anglo-Russian *entente cordiale* led to an at least "informal" co-cordination of actions vis-à-vis Poland and the French candidate to the Polish throne, Prince Conti, in the fall of 1697. The forthcoming British attitude toward the tsar who intended to escalate the war against Turkey, the ally of France, could not but have an impact on Constantinople at a time when the affairs of the Ottoman Empire were of utmost concern to the diplomatic chanceries of Europe. In the eyes of sophisticated Englishmen, keeping the Sublime Porte out of the heartlands of Europe implied the weakening of French influence in the area. Writing in 1705, Burnet justified the use of Saxon troops in Poland by Augustus in order to frustrate the French intention "to turn that free and elective state into a hereditary and absolute dominion. Under the pretence of civil war, like to arise at home, on the Prince Conti's account, *and of the war with the Turks,* he had brought in an army of Saxons...."[192] Although aware of Polish jealousy of the Saxons and of the increased threat of foreign intervention and civil war in Poland, Burnet's "synoptic" view of the over-all balance of forces is nevertheless enlightening.

This synoptic British approach to foreign policy did not exclude flexibility. It made Peter's Utrecht proposal for a broadly based political, military and commercial cooperation most welcome and feasible without depriving William of an alternative diplomacy aimed at separating Turkey from France via peace with the Habsburg Empire and its allies, including Muscovy. In fact, cordial relations with Russia might prod the Porte to prefer London's advice to that of Paris.

The history of the short-lived first anti-French Anglo-Russian *entente* also shows that British utilization of the tsar's Utrecht address and of the Muscovite hopes attached to it does not bear out the exaggerated claims of Marx according to whom "even before the epoch of Anne, at the very epoch of Russian ascendancy in Europe, springing up at the time of Peter I., the plans

of Russia were understood" by British statesmen, who allegedly
connived in them and betrayed England's own allies, such as
Sweden, to Russia. But if the "Russianism" of Dutch and English statesmen whom, in the words of Marx, "Peter I had en-
trapped during his stay at Amsterdam and the Hague in 1697,
[and] whom he afterwards directed by his ambassadors"[193]
cannot be substantiated, the tsar's encounter with William at
Utrecht and his subsequent visit to England also refutes Leonid
A. Nikiforov's contrasting thesis, set forth in reference to Peter's
intention to conclude an alliance with England. According to
the Soviet historian, "The English government did not wish to
contribute in any way to the strengthening of Russia and did
not want to assist the Russian government in the implementation of its plan to obtain an outlet to the sea and to conduct
independent trade with European states."[194] To develop commercial relations with Western Europe via the Baltic, Nikiforov
suggests, the Russian government attempted again and again to
enter into an alliance with England but these offers were de-
clined.[195] However, to quote a British historian writing about
royal marriage negotiations at the opening of the seventeenth
century, "The basic principle of English policy towards Russia,
consistent for nearly half a century, had been to avoid any kind
of political entanglement with Moscow."[196] Although Anglo-
Russian relations deteriorated in the seventeenth century, especially in the wake of the execution of Charles I condemned in
Muscovy, and the restoration of the Stuarts failed to bring
about the hoped-for reinstatement of the British merchants'
earlier trading privileges in Russia,[197] the cordiality of the encounter at Utrecht held out a promise in this respect, too.

Despite the deterioration of British-Russian relations in Peter's
last years, English merchants were repeatedly assured that they
could ply their trade undisturbed. Subsequently, during the
Polish War of Succession in the mid-1730's, when circumstances
had changed again, Russia's first, and as Dietrich Gerhard noted,

for several decades only, formal commercial treaty with a foreign power was concluded with England in 1734. It was followed, after four years of at times difficult negotiations, by the signing of an anti-French military-political alliance of the two countries ratified in 1743. It is noteworthy that the first British draft stipulated no time limit for the treaty and also the incorporation of the earlier trade agreement into it. To be sure, the alliance came to naught as a result of the "Diplomatic Revolution of 1756" and the Seven Years War because England supported Prussia, whereas Russia sided with France and Austria. It is nevertheless of interest that the basic assumption of the first Anglo-Russian political treaty was that in case of a war, Russia was to help Britain with troops, while the latter would support her Eastern ally with ships—an idea implicit in Peter's Utrecht address and his visit to England.[198]

The friendly understanding attained in the first exchanges between Peter and William in Holland, and further strengthened, symbolically, by the latter's gift of a newly built British ship to the tsar culminated in Peter's visit to England. The *entente* lasted for about seven months, from September, 1697 to April, 1698. The first signs of trouble appeared two weeks before Peter returned to Holland, when he learned Vienna's inclination to consider the idea of a separate peace with Constantinople through William's mediation. Yet in the absence of details about the secret negotiations, Peter's caveat given to William on the occasion of his farewell to him, was kept within the bounds of friendship. This interpretation is borne out by both the gracious reply sent by the tsar to William's subsequent apologetic explanation for the clandestine nature of his mediation between the emperor and the sultan[199] and by a passage in P. P. Shafirov's famous analysis of "The Just Causes of the War Between Sweden and Russia" published with Peter's editorial assistance and approval, nearly twenty years later. Accordingly,

> . . . his Czarish Majesty during his stay in *England*, was warned by
> the Court, not to pass through the Swedish Territories, and Intima-
> tions were given him, that he had great Dangers to apprehend for
> his own high Person: The King of *Great Britain* himself offered to
> his Czarish Majesty a Convoy by Sea to Archangel, in case he should
> not think it safe to travel by Land.[200]

Regardless of the propagandistic nature of Shafirov's important work which was translated into English[201] and the self-
serving list of anti-Swedish grievances contained in it, the cita-
tion above shows that elements of the first Anglo-Russian *entente* survived the tsar's initial disappointment with William and
Russian resentment was directed primarily against the emperor.
Indeed it was only the Treaty of Carlowitz which definitely
eliminated the British need for further Russian pressure on Constantinople;[202] henceforth, it was Peter who often needed, and
availed himself of, London's good offices at the Sublime Porte,
and Stockholm, too.[203]

Actually, it was William III who first offered to mediate between Sweden and Russia in 1700. After William's death, and
Peter's defeat at Narva, the tables were turned and the tsar
would have liked to persuade England to prod Charles XII into
peace negotiations, even offering to join the Grand Alliance of
the Maritime Powers and Austria. Perhaps it was the failure of
these efforts[204] that motivated Peter to consider Louis XIV for
the role of the mediator via Rákóczi.[205] The Warsaw treaty of
1707 entered into with the Hungarian prince, a leader of rebels
against the emperor, constituted a reversal of Peter's former
alliance with Vienna and *entente cordiale* with England. Willing
to fight "under the Banner of England" in William's war against
France, the common foe, ten years earlier, the tsar, humiliated
by the Swedes at Narva in the meantime, was now ready to send
his troops against the Grand Alliance to defend Russia's interests
in Central Europe. Devoid of the romantic notions reflected in
the Utrecht address, the foredoomed move was a dramatic

illustration of how tortuous Petrine diplomacy tended to follow, by design or oversight, the advice given by the ill-fated Livonian nobleman, Johan Reinhold Patkul, to Augustus of Saxony shortly after the latter's first meeting with the tsar. Accordingly, diplomatic negotiators should be guided, above all, by the rule *nesciat sinistra quid faciat dextra.* Characteristically, the same memorandum proposing a joint Polish-Danish-Muscovite "enterprise" against Sweden also stressed the desirability of impressing upon "brothers-compatriots" (*Mitbrüder und verwandten*) in Livonia that they would be liberated rather than subjugated ("*dass es angesehen sey sie zu liberiren und nicht zu subjugieren*").[206]

Naturally, this last fine point, frequently stressed in propaganda, was not always followed through in practice by either Russia or the other powers of the international system which she was about to join at the time of Peter's first encounter with William at Utrecht. Herein lies the irony. Indeed, one is almost tempted to paraphrase the Italian adage by saying that if it had not in fact been given, the "Muscovy Czar's Speech" should have been invented for the benefit of the student of history.

APPENDIX

1. First French edition of the tsar's Utrecht address to William III printed in London, 1697. Courtesy British Library, London: 616 m 23 (106). Cf. pp. 5, 8-12, and 39 above.

2. The French versions of 1721 and 1742 of Peter's speech as published side-by-side by M. A Venevitinov in Moscow, 1897. Cf. pp. 2, 8-13, 17-18 above.

3. Facsimiles of the title page of the 1742 French biography of Peter I by Eléazar de Mauvillon (a copy of which was in Voltaire's possession) and of the tsar's speech. Cf. p. 13 above and note 23 below.

4. The English summary of the Utrecht encounter as printed on p. 38 of *The Metalic History of the Three Last Reigns* appended to vol. IV (1744) of *The History of England*. Written by Mr. [Paul de] Rapin de Thoyras. Translated into English with Additional Notes by N. Tindal. 2d ed., 4 vols. (London, 1732-47). Cf. pp. 9 and 17 above and illustration no. 3.

[handwritten annotations: K. Peter I... E 90   816 m 23   168   106]

Compliment du Grand C Z A R de Moſcovie, au R O I de la Grand' Bretagne, a Utrecht.

57

T RES-RENOMMÉ EMPEREUR.

Ce n'a point été le deſir de voir les Villes Fameuſes de l'Empire d'Allemagne, ou la plus Puiſſante Republique de l'Univers, qui m'a fait laiſſer mon Trône & mes Armées Victorieuſes pour venir dans un Pays éloigné ; ça été uniquement la Vehemente Paſſion de Viſiter le plus Brave & le plus Genereux Heros du Siècle.

J'ai mon Souhait accompli, & je ſuis ſuffiſamment recompencé pour mon Voyage d'avoir joüi de Votre Preſence. Votre doux Accueil m'a donné plus de Satisfaction que la Priſe d'Aſoph & le Triomphe ſur les Tartares : L'Honneur de la Conqueſte vous appartient : Votre Genie Martial a conduit mon Épée, & la Noble Emulation de vos Exploits ont inſpiré dans mon Cœur les premieres Penſées que J'ai eu d'aggrandir mon Empire.

Je n'ai point de Termes pour exprimer la Veneration que J'ai pour Votre Perſonne Sacrée, mon Voyage ſans Pareil en eſt une Preuve.

La Saiſon eſt ſi avancée, & J'eſpere que la Paix l'eſt auſſi, que Je n'aurai pas l'occaſion, que Maximilien a eu, de Combatre ſous la Banniere d'Angleterre contre la France, le Commun, &c.

Si la Guerre continuë, Je manderai aux Generaux de mes Armées de ſe tenir prêts à ſuivre inceſſamment Vos Ordres, & ſi, ſoit en Paix, ſoit en Guerre, vos Sujets, Induſtrieux, veulent Trafiquer juſques aux Parties les plus Septentrionales du Monde, les Ports de la Ruſſie leur ſeront libres & ouverts ; Je leur accorderai des Immunitez plus grandes qu'ils n'ont encore eu juſques ici, & les ferai Enregitrer dans les plus precieux Regitres de mon Empire, pour être un Témoignage Perpetuel de l'Eſtime que J'ai pour le plus Digne des Rois.

A LONDRES,
Se Vend par C. LUCAS, demeurant dans les *Black-Fryers*, auprès de la Riviere, vis à vis de la Couronne, 1697.

1. First French edition of the tsar's Utrecht address to William III printed in London, 1697. Courtesy British Library, London: 616 m 23 (106). Cf. pp. 5, 8-12, 18, and 39 above.

ПРИЛОЖЕНІЕ III.

РѢЧЬ,

ПРИПИСЫВАЕМАЯ ПЕТРУ ВЕЛИКОМУ ИНОСТРАННЫМИ ПИСАТЕЛЯМИ
ПРИ ОПИСАНІИ ЕГО СВИДАНІЯ СЪ КОРОЛЕМЪ ВИЛЬГЕЛЬМОМЪ III
АНГЛІЙСКИМЪ, 1 СЕНТЯБРЯ 1697 Г. ВЪ УТРЕХТѢ.

По тексту анонимнаго автора Исторіи Вильгельма III, короля Великобри-
таніи (Histoire de Guillaume III, roi de la
Grande Bretagne, nouvelle édition aug-
mentée. Amsterdam 1721, tome II, page
289).

Ce n'a pas été, Sire, le désir de voir
les villes fameuses de l'Empire d'Allemagne
ou la plus puissante république de l'univers qui m'a fait laisser mon trône et mes
armées victorieuses; c'a été uniquement
la passion véhémente, que j'ai eue de voir
le plus renommé et le plus grand Héros
de ce siècle. Mon souhait est accompli et
je suis suffisament recompensé des suites
incomodes que pourrait avoir mon voyage
puisque je suis assez heureux de jouir de
Votre présence. L'acceuil, que m'a fait
Votre Majesté, m'a donné plus de satisfaction que ne m'en a donné la prise d'Azoph
et mes triomphes sur les Tartares. L'honneur de cette conquête Vous appartient,
Sire, en quelque manière. Votre génie
martial que j'ai regardé comme mon mo-
dèle, a conduit mon bras et mon épée; et
la noble émulation de Vos grands exploits
a inspiré dans mon coeur les premières
pensées d'agrandir mon Empire. Je n'ai
point de termes assez forts pour exprimer
la vénération et la haute estime que j'ai

По тексту анонимной (соч. Мовиль-
она) Исторіи Петра Великаго (Histoire
de Pierre I surnommé le Grand. Amsterdam et Leipzig, 1742, tome III, Preuves,
page 1).

Ce n'a pas tant été le désir de visiter
les célèbres villes de l'Empire de l'Allemagne et la plus puissante république de
l'univers, qui m'a fait quitter le trône et
m'absenter de mes armées victorieuses,
que celui de voir le plus brave héros du
siècle. Ce désir est satisfait et je recueille
les fruits de mon voyage en me trouvant
admis en Votre Royale présence. Vos généreux et tendres embrassements m'ont
fait plus de plaisir que la prise d'Azoph et
mes victoires sur les Tartares; mais je Vous
suis redevable de la Conquête de cette
importante clé de la Mer Noire. C'est Votre esprit martial qui a dirigé mon épée.
L'émulation de Vos exploits a fait naître
en mon coeur la première pensée d'agrandir mes Etats. Ma vénération pour Votre
personne Sacrée est au-dessus de toute
expression. Ce voyage même n'en est qu'
une faible preuve. La saison est si avancée
et la Paix de l'Europe est sur un tel pié,
que je n'ose me flatter de l'avantage et de
l'occasion que je voudrais avoir de com-

2. The French versions of 1721 and 1742 of Peter's speech as published side-by-side
by M. A. Venevitinov in Moscow, 1897. Cf. pp. 2, 8-13, 17-18 above.

pour Votre personne sacrée; mon voyage qui n'a pas d'exemple en est une preuve. La saison est si avancée et d'ailleurs la paix qui se négocie est si prochaine, que je n'aurai pas l'occasion qu'eut l'Empereur Maximilien, de combattre sous les étendarts d'Angleterre contre la France, la commune ennemie de la chretienté. Si la guerre continue cependant, je donnerai ordre aux généraux de mes Armées de se tenir prets de suivre incessament les Votres; et soit en paix, soit en guerre, si Vos sujets industrieux veulent trafiquer jusqu'aux parties les plus septentrionales du monde, les portes de la Russie leur seront ouvertes. Je leur accorderai des immunités plus grandes que celles qu'ils ont eues jusqu'ici; et je les ferai insérer dans les plus précieux régistres de mon Empire pour être un témoignage perpétuel de l'estime que j'ai pour le plus grand et le plus digne de tous les Rois.

battre sous Vos étendarts. Cependant, s[i] la guerre continuait, je suis prêt à suivre Vos ordres avec mon Armée; et soit en temps de paix ou de guerre, si Vos ingénieux sujets veulent négocier par toute l'étendue de mes Etats, tous les ports leur y seront ouverts et ils jouiront de plus grands privilèges et immunités que ceux dont jouissent actuellement les plus favorisés des Etrangers dans quelques unes de mes places et qu'aucuns autres ayent eus avant eux. Et ces privilèges et immunités seront enregistrées authentiquement dans les plus prècieux Annales de mon Empire, en témoignage de la vénération et de cette estime que j'ai et que j'aurai toujours pour le plus digne des Rois.

2. The French versions of Peter's speech continued.

HISTOIRE
DE
PIERRE I.
SURNOMMÉ
LE GRAND,
EMPEREUR
DE TOUTES LES
RUSSIES.

ROI DE SIBERIE, DE CASAN, D'ASTRACAN,
GRAND DUC DE MOSCOVIE, &c. &c. &c.

Enrichie de Plans de Batailles & de Médailles.

A AMSTERDAM ET A LEIPZIG,
Chez ARKSTEE ET MERKUS,
MDCCXLII.

3. Facsimile of the title page of the 1742 French biography of Peter I by Eléazar de Mauvillon (a copy of which was in Voltaire's possession). Cf. p. 13 above and note 23 below.

PREUVES

DE

L'HISTOIRE

DE

PIERRE I.

EMPEREUR

DE TOUTES LES

RUSSIES.

DISCOURS DU CZAR AU ROI D'ANGLETERRE.

TRES RENOMME' MONARQUE,

CE n'a pas tant été le desir de visiter les célèbres Villes de l'Empire d'Allemagne, & la plus puissante République de l'Univers, qui m'a fait quiter le Trône, & m'absenter de mes Armées victorieuses, que celui de voir le plus brave Héros du siecle. Ce desir est satisfait, & je recueille les fruits de mon voyage en me trouvant admis en Votre Royale Présence. Vos généreux & tendres embrassemens m'ont fait plus de plaisir, que la prise d'Azoph, & mes victoires sur les Tartares; mais je vous suis redevable de la conquête de cette importan- te olé de la Mer Noire. C'est votre génie martial qui a dirigé mon épée. L'émulation de vos exploits a fait naitre en mon cœur la prémiere pensée d'agrandir mes Etats. Ma vénération pour Votre Personne Sacrée est au-dessus de toute expression. Ce voyage même n'en est qu'une foible preuve. La saison est si avancée, & la Paix de l'Europe est sur un tel pié, que je n'ose me flatter de l'avantage & de l'occasion que je voudrois avoir de combattre sous vos étendarts. Cependant, si la guerre continuoit, je suis prêt à suivre vos ordres avec mon Armée; & soit en tems de Paix ou de Guerre, si vos ingénieux sujets veulent négocier par toute l'étendue de mes Etats, tous les ports leur y sont ouverts, & ils y jouiront de plus granas

3. Facsimile of the tsar's speech. Cf. p. 13 above and note 23 below.

grands privilèges & immunités que ceux
dont jouissent actuellement les plus favorisés
des Etrangers dans quelques-unes de mes
Places, & qu'aucuns autres ayent eu avant
eux. Et ces privilèges & immunités seront
enrégistrées autentiquement dans les plus pré-
cieuses Annales de mon Empire, en témoignage de la vénération & de cette estime
que j'ai & que j'aurai toujours pour le plus
digne des Rois.

Après que le Czar eut pris des enga-
gemens avec le Roi de Pologne contre
Charles XII, il chercha tous les moyens
de faire querelle à ce dernier, & se plai-
gnit d'abord assez doucement qu'on ne lui
voit point rendu à Riga les honneurs qui
lui étoient dus, lorsqu'il y avoit passé
vec ses Ambassadeurs. Le Roi de Suède
informé de ces plaintes, écrivit au Comte
e Dahlberg, alors Gouverneur de Riga
& Capitaine-Général de la Livonie, pour
qu'il eût à envoyer une relation de ce qui
'étoit passé lors de l'arrivée du Czar à
Riga, afin qu'on sût la satisfaction qu'on
ouvoit lui offrir au cas qu'on eût man-
ué à son égard, & afin que cette affaire
accommodât à l'amiable. Sur quoi le
omte de Dahlberg écrivit la Lettre sui-
ante à Charles XII.

LETTRE

pologétique du Comte Eric de Dahlberg,
Maréchal-de-camp, Gouverneur-Géné-
ral de Livonie, au Roi de Suède, *écrite*
de Riga *le 18. Mars 1700, & traduite*
sur l'Original Latin.

SIRE,

PLus il me paroissoit important à la
Suède de vivre en bonne amitié avec

„ la Moscovie, plus il me sembloit néces-
„ saire de recevoir d'une maniere distin-
„ guée la grande Ambassade du Czar;
„ & je me faisois un vrai plaisir de tout
„ préparer pour lui faire une reception
„ qui effaçât tout ce qui avoit jamais été
„ fait auparavant à l'égard des autres Am-
„ bassades Moscovites qui avoient traver-
„ sé la Livonie. J'aurois seulement sou-
„ haité que j'eusse pu revoir les ordres
„ de Votre Majesté sur plusieurs cho-
„ ses où je ne savois pas bien comment
„ je devois me conduire. Mais le tems
„ n'ayant pas permis à Votre Majesté
„ de me répondre assez tôt, je fus obli-
„ gé de consulter les Gouverneurs de Re-
„ val & de Nerva sur certains articles
„ que j'ignorois, sur-tout si c'étoit la
„ coutume de régaler solemnellement les
„ Ambassadeurs Moscovites; & sur ce
„ qu'ils me répondirent que cela ne s'é-
„ toit jamais pratiqué, & que tous les
„ Ambassadeurs Moscovites qui depuis
„ 1660 avoient passé par l'Esthonie,
„ l'Ingrie & la Livonie pour aller en
„ Suède ou ailleurs, avoient été contens
„ des honneurs accoutumés, sans préten-
„ dre qu'on leur donnât des festins pu-
„ blics, je résolus de me conformer à
„ cela quant à ce point. Du reste je
„ n'oubliai rien pour faire une reception
„ des plus honorables à l'Ambassade, &
„ pour surpasser même mes prédécesseurs
„ à cet égard. Je fis partir le Colonel
„ Glasenap, avec un Capitaine nommé
„ Dornfeld, & plusieurs autres Officiers
„ qui parloient la Langue Moscovite, &
„ leur commandai de se rendre à Nyhuis
„ à l'extrémité de la Livonie, pour y at-
„ tendre l'Ambassade du Czar. J'ordon-
„ nai en même tems aux Magistrats des
„ environs, de faire des provisions & de

Rr 3   „ les

3.Facsimile of the tsar's speech continued.

The exergue contains only the Engraver's name.

Reverse : Europe with an olive branch in one hand, and a horn of plenty in the other, is sitting on the sea-shore, where several ships are seen at sea under sail. In the exergue is only this word :

ÉUROPA.

Europe.

2. The Plenipotentiaries of the several powers who concluded the peace shut the temple of Janus, as appears from the inscription over the gate :

JANO SACRUM.
Dedicated to Janus.

Before it is an altar, at the foot of which lies a sow, just immolated : The legend is borrowed from this line of Virgil, Æn. VIII. ver. 641.

CÆSA CONFIRMANT FŒDERA PORCA.
They confirm their alliance by the sacrifice of a sow.

In order to understand this, it must be observed, that antiently among the Romans, the Sabines, and the nations of Germany, they used to confirm alliances by sacrificing a sow : Which custom Livy (Lib. 1. Cap. xxiv.) traces up as high as the first treaty entered into by the Romans, which was that they made with the people of Alba. The Priest, in whose presence the two nations swore to perform the treaty, said, *let he who shall first break this treaty, be so struck by Jupiter, as I shall strike this sow,* and upon that he killed the victim.

The reverse contains in a ring round the medal, the arms of the Emperor, KEYRER, Spain, SPANGIEN, Brandeburg, BRANDENBURG, the Palatinate, PALTZ, Saxony, SAXEN, Bavaria, BEYEREN, England, ENGELAND, Sweden, SWEDEN ; of the seven Provinces, 7. PROVINCIEN, the Spanish Netherlands, SPAANSCHE NEDERLANDEN, the Empire, T'RYK, Lorrain, LOTHARINGEN, Savoy, SAVOYEN, and France, VRANCKRYK. In the middle of the field is the palace of Ryswick, and this legend round it :

RYSWICK, GUILLELMI III, DEI GRATIA, MAGNÆ BRITANNIÆ ETC. REGIS PALATIUM.
Ryswick, the palace of William III, by the grace of God, King of Great-Britain, &c.

The date is in the exergue :

MDCXCVII.

3. The arms of the village of Ryswick set against a trophy, with this inscription in the round :

PAX RYSWICCENSIS.
The peace of Ryswick.

In the exergue :

1697.

Reverse : Peace sitting, holding an olive branch in one hand, and a horn of plenty in the other : With this legend :

PAX PUBLICA.
The general peace.

4. The glorious success of King William, who by his courage and conduct, and by the assistance of the Dutch, as well as by the concurrence and affection of the British Nation, weary of the arbitrary proceedings of James II, had found means to get himself acknowledged the lawful King of Great-Britain, spread his reputation throughout all Europe, even to the remotest parts of the North. So that the Czar of Muscovy not only sent a solemn embassy to the Republic of the United Provinces, to testify his esteem for them, but would also go thither himself. He went incognito

with the Ambassadors, and had an interview with King William at Utrecht, September the 11, 1697, on which occasion the Czar gave him the greatest tokens of esteem : He told his British Majesty, that the desire he had to see him was the only and true motive of the great and difficult journey he had undertaken ; and not the curiosity to travel through the several countries of Europe, in order to admire the wonders of them. That he preferred above the conquest of Azoph, the defeat of the Tartars, and all his victories, the happiness of seeing a Prince, whose heroic actions first inspired him with a desire to signalize himself by extending the limits of his Dominions at the expence of his enemies, and that the King was therefore to be considered as the first cause of the Czar's triumphs. The present medal was struck on occasion of this extraordinary interview.

The front represents the King's bust crowned with laurel, and this legend round it :

GUILELMUS III, DEI GRATIA, MAGNÆ BRITANNIÆ, FRANCIÆ, ET HIBERNIÆ REX, FIDEI DEFENSOR, PIUS, AUGUSTUS.
William III, by the grace of God, King of Great Britain, France and Ireland, defender of the faith, pious, august.

Reverse : The King receiving the Czar at the gate of his palace, with these words in the rim :

SIC OLIM HEROES.
Thus acted the ancient heroes.

The city of Utrecht is seen in the offings. In the exergue is the following inscription.

PETRI ALEXIEWICZ CZAR MAGNIQUE GUILELMI REGIS AMICITIA TRAJECTI AD RHENUM, XI. SEPTEMBRIS, MDCXCVII.
The friendly interview between the Czar Peter Alexiewicz and King William the Great, at Utrecht, September 11, 1697.

All the following medals in this plate were struck on a very melancholy occasion, I mean the death of the great King William.

5. In the middle of the field is the King's bust, crowned with laurel, and this inscription round it :

GULIELMUS III, DEI GRATIA, BRITANNIÆ REX, ARAUSIONENSIUM PRINCEPS, BELGII GUBERNATOR.
William III, by the grace of God, King of Great Britain, Prince of Orange, and Governor of Holland.

Round the bust are set down in five circles the names of the twenty-five Kings of England, from Egbert the Saxon King, to Stephen, who died in the year 1154. Their characters are expressed by the planets, and on one side of their names is the date of their accession to the throne, and on the other the year of their death. We shall set down here their names, with the dates annexed. As to the planets expressing their respective characters, we shall just name them ; but as we do not pretend to any skill in judicial astrology, we shall leave it to those who are acquainted with that wonderful science, to shew how the character of each King is justly expressed by the planet affixed to his name.

Began to Reign.	Names of the Kings.	Planets.	Died.
801.	EGBERT Roi Saxon. EGBERT a Saxon King.	Sol or the Sun.	838.
838.	ETHELWOLF.	Jupiter.	858.
858.	ETHELBALD.	Luna.	800.
860.	ETHELBERT.	Luna.	866.
866.	ETHELRED.	Mars.	872.
872.	ALFRED.	Sol.	900.
			901. 70.

4. The English summary of the Utrecht encounter as printed on p. 38 of *The Metalic History of the Three Last Reigns* appended to vol. IV of *The History of England.* Written by Mr. [Paul de] Rapin de Thoyras. Translated into English with Additional Notes by N. Tindal. 2d ed., 4 vols. (London, 1732-47). Cf. pp. 9 and 17 above and illustration no. 3.

NOTES

1. Leo Loewenson, "The First Interviews between Peter I and William III in 1697: Some Neglected English Material," *The Slavonic and East European Review*, XXXVI (1957-58), 308-16.

2. Ibid., p. 308. For the date and the problems relevant to its clarification, cf. note 1 and the references in it. At the time of the meeting, the Julian calendar was still in force in England, hence the double dates, according to the Old and New Styles. In the following, they will be given according to the New Style (N.S.).

3. Ibid., p. 309; M. A. Venevitinov, *Russkie v Gollandii* (Moscow, 1897), App. III, pp. 197-98. For the older literature, see J. Scheltema, *Anecdotes historiques sur Pierre-le-Grand et sur ses voyages en Hollande et a Zaandam dans les années 1697 et 1717.* Traduit du hollandais par N. P. Muilman (Lausanne, 1842), pp. 120-21, n. 2. Twentieth century Dutch authors take a similarly skeptical attitude. Cf. Boris Raptschinsky, *Peter de Groote in Holland in 1697-1698: een historische schets* (Dissertatie Amsterdam G.U., 1925), pp. 103-104 and Th. J. G. Locher, *Peter de Grote* (Amsterdam, 1947), p. 100. For this information, I am in the debt of Mr. Volkert Groothoff, Bibliographical Department, University Library, Utrecht, and Archivist Theo Thomassen, First Section, Algemeen Rijksarchief, Gravenhage, Holland. (Letter to the author, April 29, 1988). Cf. Append. 2.

4. Venevitinov, *Russkie v Gollandii,* p. 75 n. 1; M. M. Bogoslovskii, *Petr I: Materialy dlya biografii,* 5 vols. (Moscow, 1940-48), II, 162, n. 3.

5. Loewenson, "The First Interviews," pp. 311, 313, 315-16.

6. Ibid., pp. 310-12 and especially no. 19. Cf. Append. 1.

7. Ibid., pp. 310-11 and n. 15.

8. Among the recent works which touch on the Utrecht meeting and Peter's visit to England but seem to ignore the article, see Nesca A. Robb,

William of Orange, 2 vols. (New York, 1962), II, 424-25; Stephen B. Baxter, *William III and the Defense of European Liberty 1650-1702* (Westport, Conn., 1966), p. 363; M. S. Anderson, *Peter the Great* (London, 1978), p. 42; Ian Grey, *Peter the Great,* Sixth Printing (Philadelphia-New York, n.d.), p. 109. Henri and Barbara van der Zee, *William and Mary* (London, 1973), pp. 427-28, is an exception. Reinhard Wittram's superb biography, *Peter I, Czar und Kaiser,* 2 vols. (Göttingen, 1964), I, 155-56, also registers Loewenson's work.

9. Loewenson, "The First Interviews," pp. 312-13.

10. For brief references in older works, cf. N. G. Ustrialov, *Istoriya tsarstvovaniya Petra Velikago,* 6 vols. (St. Petersburg, 1858-63), III, 89; S. M. Soloviev, *Istoriya Rossii s drevneishikh vremen,* 15 vols. (Moscow, 1960-66), XIII, 554; Karl Stählin, *Geschichte Russlands,* 4 vols. (Graz, 1961), II, 41; K. Waliszewski, *Peter the Great,* 2d ed. (London, 1898), p. 93; Michael T. Florinsky, *Russia. A History and An Interpretation,* 2 vols. (New York, Tenth Printing, 1965), I, 321; V. O. Kluchevsky, *A History of Russia,* transl. C. J. Hogarth, 5 vols. (New York, 1911-31), IV, 21; Eugene Schuyler, *Peter the Great,* 2 vols. (New York, 1890), I, 293. For the Treaty of Ryswick and its implications, see J. S. Bromley, ed., *The Rise of Great Britain and Russia,* vol. VI of *The New Cambridge Modern History* (Cambridge, 1970), pp. 252-53, 381-88, 582 and passim.

11. "The Czar of Muscovys Speech." *Dep. 313/XV. Box 1. Miscellanea, Sutherland Archives.* Department of Manuscripts, National Library of Scotland, Edinburgh. I am grateful to Elizabeth, Countess of Sutherland, for permitting me to do research in the family papers in Edinburgh and to publish the transcript of the document.

12. For collating my transcript of the text with the handwritten original, I am in the debt of Dr. Thomas I. Rae, Keeper, and Mrs. Olive Geddes, compiler of the inventory of the Sutherland Papers, both from the Department of Manuscripts, National Library of Scotland, Edinburgh.

13. Giles E. Dawson and Laetitia Kennedy-Skipton, *Elizabethan Handwriting* (New York, 1966), pp. 16, 23. For calling my attention to the book just cited, I am in the debt of Professor Gunnar Boklund, Chairman of the Department of English at the University of Denver.

14. Narcissus Luttrell, *A Brief Historical Relation of State Affairs from September 1678 to April 1714,* 6 vols. (Oxford, 1857), IV, 291 (cited henceforth as *Diary*); Loewenson, "The First Interviews," pp. 310,

312. For Narcissus Luttrell (1657-1721), an annalist and bibliographer, and his day-by-day chronicle of contemporary events, cf. *DNB*, XXXIV (1893), 300-301.

15. Loewenson, "The First Interviews," pp. 309, n. 7 and 312-13, n. 20. Cf. ill. no. 3 and append. no. 4.

16. *A Sermon Preached before the King at Whitehall*, On the Second of December, 1697. Being the Day of Thanksgiving for the Peace. By the Right Reverend Father in God, Gilbert, Lord Bishop of Sarum (London, 1698), p. 13.

17. Loewenson, "The First Interviews," pp. 311-12 and n. 17.

18. James Cracraft, *The Church Reform of Peter the Great* (Stanford, 1971), pp. 28-32.

19. For Burnet and his relationship with William, cf. Robb, *William of Orange*, II, 240-42, 290, 304, 363, 365, 416, 435.

20. For the contemporary phrase " . . . the preservation of the peace and liberties of Europe, from the ambitious designs of the common enemy," see the letter of Sir Joseph Williamson, one of the British plenipotentiaries at Ryswick, to the Duke of Shrewsbury, England's secretary of state, in William Coxe, *Private and Original Correspondence of Charles Talbot, Duke of Shrewsbury, with King William, the Leaders of the Whig Party, and Other Distinguished Statesmen* (London, 1821), p. 362 (Hague, Aug. 6-16, 1697).

21. Loewenson, "The First Interviews," p. 312.

22. *Oeuvres complètes de Voltaire*, 92 vols. (Kehl, 1785), XXVII, 6-7.

23. In a letter dated November 17, 1761, the Countess Sabina von Bassewitz sent Voltaire a list of works dealing with Peter I and Russia. It included Eléazar de Mauvillon's *Histoire de Pierre I, surnommé le grand empereur de toutes les Russies*, published in Amsterdam in 1742, which contained the third French version of Peter's speech mentioned above. Theodore Besterman, ed., *The Complete Works of Voltaire. Correspondence and related documents.* Definitive edition, 50 vols. (Geneva-Banbury, Oxfordshire, 1968-77), XXIV, 122-23 (D10159). Cited hereafter as *Voltaire. Correspondence.* Cf. Append 2 and 3.

24. Voltaire, *Histoire de Russie*, pp. 143-44. Voltaire repeatedly refers to both Perry and Lefort's manuscripts. Ibid., pp. 135-36, 141, 146-48, 150, 153. Cf. John Perry, *The State of Russia under the Present Czar* (New

York, reprint of 1968), p. 163; Moritz Posselt, *Der General und Admiral Franz Lefort*, 2 vols. (Frankfurt on the Main, 1866), II, 420.

25. Loewenson, "The First Interviews," pp. 308-313-15.

26. Posselt, *Lefort*, II, 599 and 601. Append. VIII and IX. See also Bogoslovskii, *Petr I*, II, 54-56, 124 and n. 1, 467-70. As noted by Ustrialov, Peter asked for the Dutch-speaking British vice-admiral Mitchell to be with him during his sojourn in England. *Istoriya Petra Velikago*, III, 97, 602. Cf. Luttrell, *Diary*, IV, 335, 357, 359, 362.

27. Venevitinov, *Russkie v Gollandii*, p. 75, n. 1. For the limitations of Peter's knowledge of Dutch, cf. Wittram, *Peter I*, I, 146 and 426, n. 43.

28. The salutation and the first half sentence of Peter's speech cited by Sir John Barrow is identical with the English text of the Edinburgh copy but the remaining five lines of the first paragraph seem to follow the French edition of 1697. John Barrow, *The Life of Peter the Great*. With explanatory notes by Henry Ketcham (New York, 1903), p. 66. Cf. Loewenson, "The First Interviews," p. 312, n. 18.

29. Ibid., pp. 312-13.

30. Robb, *William of Orange*, II, 424.

31. Venevitinov, *Russkie v Gollandii*, pp. 72-73.

32. Ibid., pp. 28-41; Avis Bohlen, "Changes in Russian Diplomacy Under Peter the Great," *Cahiers du Monde Russe et Soviétique*, VII (1966), 342-45; Bogoslovskii, *Petr I*, II, 7-15.

33. Ibid., pp. 162-63 and n. 3; 163-64 and n. 2.

34. For a summary of the terms of the Treaty of Ryswick, cf. David Ogg, *Europe in the 17th Century*, 6th, rev. ed. (London, 1954), pp. 258-59. See also n. 65 below.

35. Bromley, *The Rise of Great Britain and Russia*, p. 621 and passim; Ogg, *Europe in the 17th Century*, p. 269. For French approaches to Maximilian and his brother, the Elector-Archbishop of Cologne as early as 1694, cf. Baxter, *William III*, pp. 317-18. See also John P. Spielman, *Leopold I of Austria* (London, 1977), pp. 96, 99, 115-16, 125-27, 136-38, 142, 149, 152, 165, 170-71, 183, 191-95, and Max Braubach, "Graf Dominik Andreas Kaunitz (1655-1705) als Diplomat," in Heinrich Fichtenau and Erich Zöllner, eds., *Beiträge zur neueren Geschichte Österreichs*, XX (1974), 231, 235, 238-40. See also n. 180 and pertinent text below.

35a. I am grateful for a critical comment expressed by Professor Stephen B. Baxter, of the University of North Carolina (Chapel Hill), suggesting that the Maximilian mentioned in the tsar's Utrecht speech was a reference to Emperor Maximilian I rather than to the Bavarian prince, because it was the emperor who fought for Henry VIII against France in the famous Battle of the Spurs (or Guinegate) in 1513. Yet while this incident may have been embedded in the historical consciousness of Western Europe, and while Maximilian I did indeed receive a sizable sum (100,000 gold crowns) from the King of England for his military assistance after the battle, such an interpretation runs into several difficulties. First, neither of the earliest and contemporary English or French texts (1697) refers to Maximilian as "emperor": as indicated above, only one later French text (1721) uses this adjective, which may be an interpolation caused precisely by the desire to "exonerate" the Bavarian prince retrospectively as that time he was a French ally. The term "Fighting under the Banner of England against France the Common" certainly could imply, at least theoretically, that Peter knew that it was Henry VIII who footed the bill of the campaign of 1513. But this assumption overlooks the fact that the English king was inexperienced and the emperor was the commander-in-chief: Maximilian I conducted the military operations in person and the British royal couple expressed their gratitude for the emperor's help in effusive terms after the joint victory over France. (Cf. Hermann Wiesflecker, *Kaiser Maximilian I,* 4 vols. [Munich, 1971-81], IV, 124-29 and 546-47, especially note 73. See also Glenn Elwood Waas, *The Legendary Character of Kaiser Maximilian* [New York, 1941, reprint of 1966], pp. 70-71 and 84-85.)

It is also difficult to substantiate the hypothesis that the Battle of the Spurs was well known in late seventeenth century Muscovy or that Peter was aware of the exact relationship between Henry and Maximilian I and alluded to it in an effort to underline his own devotion to William III. The only person in his entourage who might have suggested such a historical analogy 184 years after the event was Francis Lefort, the official leader of the Muscovite embassy. But the papers of both the general and those of his nephew, Louis Lefort, who was the secretary of the Russian delegation at the time, are silent about the tsar's speech at Utrecht. If it could be proved that the Maximilian mentioned in the Utrecht address was the emperor who won the Battle of the Spurs, the hypothesis would enhance the argument that the tsar's speech was "embellished" by some knowledgeable person close to William III, who wanted to reinforce the idea of the need for a European-wide coalition against Louis XIV by incorporating in Peter's address the earlier historical analogy. In the absence of further evidence, however, I find the reference to Maximilian Emmanuel more immediate and plausible.

36.   Philip Longworth, *Alexis* (New York, 1984), pp. 132-34, 245-49; Max J. Okenfuss, "Technical Training in Russia under Peter the Great," *History of Education Quarterly*, XIII (1973), 327 passim.

37.   Baxter, *William III*, p. 363 (". . . the Tsar could talk of nothing but the Navy and carpentry, neither of which interested William III,"); Leonard Krieger, *Kings and Philosophers, 1689-1789*) (New York, 1970), pp. 46-47 ("The guise was more truthful than the reality, for the artisan-tsar went more as an artisan than as a tsar. . . . This addiction to the instrument, the means, the procedure, rather than the system, the theory, or the process was to characterize his whole regime.").

38.   Bishop Burnet's *History of His Own Time: With Notes by the Earle of Dartmouth and Hardwicke, Speaker Onslow, and Dean Swift*, 2d enlarged ed., 6 vols. (Oxford, 1833), IV, 407; also ibid., p. 408: "He (the tsar) was desirous to understand our doctrine, but he did not seem disposed to mend matters in Muscovy;". Cf. Cracraft, *The Church Reform of Peter the Great*, p. 36 and n. 1.

39.   Voltaire, *Histoire de l'Empire de Russie*, p. 149.

40.   *The Diary of General Patrick Gordon*, no. 3, in *Russia Through European Eyes*, General Editor A. G. Cross (London-Edinburgh, 1968), pp. 170-74 and passim; Wittram, *Peter I*, I, 126; Posselt, *Lefort*, I, 519-20.

41.   Cited ibid., I, 518-19. Emphasis in the original.

42.   Bogoslovskii, *Petr I*, I, 145. *Pereiaslavskoe Ozero*, mentioned by Bogoslovskii, is also called Pleshcheevo Lake. It is in the Southwestern part of Iaroslavl *Oblast'*, Northeast of Moscow. Cf. *Great Soviet Encyclopedia*, 25 vols. (New York-London, 1973-81), II, 223d.

43.   Robert K. Massie, *Peter the Great* (New York, 1980), p. 197.

44.   Bogoslovskii, *Petr I*, II, 79-81, 88-96, 99.

45.   Ibid., II, 98.

46.   Ibid., II, 9, 10-11; Ustrialov, *Istoriya Petra Velikago*, III, 16, n. 26. For the text of the Treaty of Alliance between Russia, the Holy Roman Empire and the Republic of Venice of January 29, 1697, see *Pis'ma i Bumagi Imperatora Petra Velikogo*, 12 vols. (St. Petersburg-Moscow,

1887-1964), I, 124-28. For the twelve points included in the instructions, cf. ibid., I, 135-37. For an English translation of the treaty, see Johann-Georg Korb, *Diary of An Austrian Secretary of Legation at the Court of Czar Peter the Great,* translated by and edited by The Count MacDonnell (London, 1863, new impression 1968), pp. 1-6. On p. 4 of this English text, the date of the "triple alliance" is erroneously given as "the 29th of January, 1698" instead of 1697.

47.   Bogoslovskii, *Petr I,* II, 9.

48.   Ibid., II, 10. Cf. Wittram, *Peter I,* I, 134, 149.

49.   Posselt, *Lefort,* II, 365-67, 400-406; Waliszewski, *Peter the Great,* p. 80. For Vienna's pertinent warnings via the Russian envoy, Kozma Nefimonov, who signed the anti-Turkish alliance with the Empire and Venice at the end of January, the first troop movements on the Russian side of the Lithuanian border and the reports of Muscovy's permanent resident in Warsaw, Aleksei Nikitin, on the Polish elections, see Ustrialov, *Istoriya Petra Velikago,* III, 16-17 and 42-53.

50.   Peter's two letters to the Cardinal-Primate of Poland and his letter to the Polish Senators and Commonwealth are printed in *Pis'ma i Bumagi,* I, 163-65, 171-72, 172 under the dates of May 31, June 2 and July 16, 1697, respectively. Cf. Burnet, *History of His Own Time,* IV, 359-61. For simultaneous reports by Sir Joseph Williamson and the British envoy at the Hague, Lord Villiers, to the Duke of Shrewsbury, indicating the impact of Conti's candidacy on the European balance of power (including the Turks) and the peace negotiations in Holland, see Coxe, *Correspondence,* pp. 341-42, 345-47 (both dated Hague, July 12, 1697). See n. 103 below.

51.   *Pis'ma i Bumagi,* I, 183-84 (July 16, 1697). Although Denmark also supported the candidacy of Augustus against Conti, the Russian requests for a closure of the Sound were refused. Sweden, which was anxious to avoid offending either Louis XIV or the tsar, took a similar position and remained neutral in the contest for the Polish crown. R. M. Hatton, *Charles XII of Sweden* (New York, 1968), pp. 102-103.

52.   Bogoslovskii, *Petr I,* II, 102-103; Ustrialov, *Istoriya Petra Velikago,* III, 53-54.

53.   *Pis'ma i Bumagi,* I, 181 (Letter to Andrei A. Vinius); Posselt, *Lefort,* II, 404-407. For the Austrian role in the election of Frederick Augustus and his conversion to Roman Catholicism, cf. Spielman, *Leopold I,*

p. 165; Max Braubach, *Prinz Eugen von Savoyen,* 5 vols. (Vienna, 1963-66), I, 245-57; Derek McKay, *Prince Eugene of Savoy* (London, 1977), p. 42.

54. Posselt, *Lefort,* II, 427-40; *Pis'ma i Bumagi,* I, 191-93, 218-22. For Sweden's role in the Nine Years War, see Ragnhild Hatton, "Gratifications and Foreign Policy: Anglo-French Rivalry in Sweden during the Nine Years War" and S. P. Oakley, "The Interception of Posts in Celle, 1694-1700," in Ragnhild Hatton and J. S. Bromley, eds., *William III and Louis XIV,* Essays 1680-1720 by and for Mark A. Thomson (Liverpool-Toronto, 1968), pp. 68-94 and 96-98, respectively. Actually, the Swedes also encouraged the Turks to continue the war against the Russians, which was in their interest, even after the Treaty of Carlowitz. Hatton, *Charles XII,* p. 105. Cf. Ustrialov, *Istoriya Petra Velikago,* III, 402-404; Bogoslovskii, *Petr I,* II, 241-43.

55. Ferdinand Grönebaum, *Frankreich in Ost-und Nordeuropa* (Wiesbaden, 1968), pp. 101-114. For previous Franco-Muscovite confrontations over Poland, going back to the times of the ephemeral Polish kingship of Henry of Valois (1573) and Tsar Ivan IV, cf. ibid., p. 123. For the significance of Poland in the alliance system of France directed against the "central powers" of Europe, i.e., the Habsburgs between the XVIth and XVIIIth centuries, cf. Marc Ferro, "Entre Paris et Moscou," *Cahiers du Monde Russe et Soviétique,* VII (1966), 359.

56. Grönebaum, *Frankreich in Ost- und Nordeuropa,* pp. 117-20; Posselt, *Lefort,* I, 227, 514-20.

57. P. Pierling, *La Russie et le Saint-Siège* (Paris, 1907), pp. 122-28.

58. Posselt, *Lefort,* II, 354-65. Until the second decade of the eighteenth century, Archangel remained the most important outlet for Russian exports (the main items of which were caviar, potash, pitch and tar). Arcadius Kahan, "Observations on Petrine Foreign Trade," *Canadian-American Slavic Studies,* VIII (1974), 228.

59. Luttrell, *Diary,* IV, 258; Posselt, *Lefort,* 419-20; Bogoslovskii, *Petr I,* II, 129-46.

60. Ibid., II, 161-62; Venevitinov, *Russkie v. Gollandii,* pp. 72-73. On September 10, Sir Joseph Williamson reported from Hague: "Myl.[ord] Villars is gone to wait on the King at Utrecht where his Ma[jes]ty has appointed to receive the Czar's ambassad[ors]s, though for my part, I would much rather wish it were to be done at Whitehall. There wants [*sic*] some

thinking in that Businesse." Williamson to Shrewsbury, Hague, Sep. 10, 1697. Public Record Office, London. SP Foreign Entry Books (SP 105), 257, fol. 339.

61.   Jake V. Th. Knoppers, "Tsar Peter I and Utrecht," *Canadian Journal of Netherlandic Studies,* I (1979), 17. From Hague, Lord Villiers reported to the Duke of Shrewsbury on August 16, 1697: "We expect the czar to be here in two or three days: the king will come hither to see him." To be sure, he added: "I believe his majesty heartily wishes the visit over; for, from what we hear, his muscovitisch majesty is but scurvy company." Coxe, *Correspondence,* p. 366. Yet within less than a month, after he "had the opportunity of seeing the czar with his majesty" at the first interview between the two "great princes" which he attended at Utrecht "in a very dirty tavern," the same plenipotentiary grudgingly admitted: "The behaviour of this man [i.e., the tsar] is very singular and capricious, though in some things he seems to have the genius of a great prince . . . ." Lord Villiers to the Duke of Shrewsbury, ibid., pp. 369-70. (Hague, Sept. 13, 1697).

62.   Marion E. Grew, *William Bentinck and William III* (London, 1924, reprint of 1971), pp. 290-93; Luttrell, *Diary,* IV, 275-76, 280; Loewenson, "The First Interviews," 314-15.

63.   *Pis'ma i Bumagi,* I, 188 (Amsterdam, Aug. 21, 1697. To Andrei A. Vinius).

64.   Robert Mandrou, *Louis XIV en son temps* (Paris, 1974), p. 498.

65.   Grew, *William Bentinck and William III,* pp. 292-94; Van der Zee, *William and Mary,* p. 427. For the intricacies regarding the diplomatic and military pressures and counterpressures surrounding the Ryswick negotiations as well as continued British concerns about French intentions, cf. the documents in Coxe, *Correspondence,* pp. 167-71, 174-75, 316-82, 540, 552, 566-67, 571-77 and passim. For the background of Leopold's reluctance to sign the treaty of Ryswick along with his allies, see Heinrich Ritter von Srbik, *Wien und Versailles 1692-1697* (Munich, 1944), especially pp. 170-316; Braubach, "Graf Dominik Andreas Kaunitz (1655-1705) als Diplomat und Staatsmann," pp. 234-35.

66.   *Pis'ma i Bumagi,* I, 208. (To Andrei A. Vinius. Amsterdam, Oct. 29, 1697). See also ibid., I, 204 (To the same, Amsterdam, Oct. 14, 1697).

67.   Van der Zee, *William and Mary,* p. 427: for the opposite view supporting my interpretation, cf. Posselt, *Lefort,* II, 420.

68.   Wittram, *Peter I*, I, 154; Bogoslovskii, *Petr I*, II, 222, 224.

69.   Ibid., II, 245-48.

70.   Cited by Posselt, *Lefort*, II, 421-22. The Russians displayed similar animosity toward Savoy whose ruler switched sides and joined Louis XIV in the last phase of the war.

71.   Waliszewski, *Peter the Great*, p. 76.

72.   Bohlen, "Changes in Russian Diplomacy," pp. 345-46. Cf. C. Bickford O'Brien, *Russia under Two Tsars 1682-1689* (Berkeley-Los Angeles, 1952), pp. 90, 100-104. For previous abortive attempts to improve Franco-Muscovite trade and perhaps even political relations in 1668, 1681 and 1682, which ended with Peter's ascent to the throne signifying the prevalence of the anti-French and anti-Catholic "Dutch party" at the tsarist court, see Andrew Lossky, "Dutch Diplomacy and the Franco-Russian Trade Negotiations in 1681," in Ragnhild Hatton and M. S. Anderson, eds., *Studies in Diplomatic History* (London, 1970), pp. 32-46 and id., "La Piquetière's Projected Mission to Moscow in 1682 and the Swedish Policy of Louis XIV," in Alan D. Ferguson and Alfred Levin, eds., *Essays in Russian History* (Hamden, Conn., 1964), pp. 71-106. But despite the tensions which arose among Denmark, Sweden and Brandenburg, the allies of France in Northern Europe, the internal turbulence in Russia and Louis XIV's exaggerated notions about Swedish strength caused the Sun King to have, in Lossky's words, "little interest in direct diplomatic relations with far-away Muscovy," nor to enter into closer relations with that state with the purpose of bringing it into his "eastern barrier" directed against the Habsburgs. Ibid., p. 94. Or, as Louis André put it, Louis XIV erroneously thought that he could deal with "Asiatic" Muscovy as he dealt with Poland or Hungary, an assumption that prevented him from winning over to his side Peter the Great. Louis André, *Louis XIV et l'Europe* (Paris, 1950), p. 352.

73.   Bogoslovskii, *Petr I*, II, 145-46; *Pis'ma i Bumagi*, I, 631 (A. A. Vinius to Peter). According to an entry in Luttrell, *Diary*, IV, 288, dated September 28, Cracow, "The new king [i.e., Augustus] has summoned all those who voted for him to appear in arms, and take the field; the cardinal primate has done the same in favour of the prince of Conti." Further, in a obvious hint at Peter, "the pope is mightily pleased at the elector of Saxony's turning Roman catholick, and has declared, that in a little time a farr greater prince will doe the same."

74. Bogoslovskii, *Petr I*, II, 166-67; Loewenson, "The First Inter-views," pp. 308-309 and 314, n. 24. For a confirmation of this part of the Polish envoy's report, see also the hitherto unpublished source in note 174 below: "Leur conversation roula sur Les affaires de Pologne, & sur La paix qui Se traitoit a Ruisvik."

75. Luttrell, *Diary*, IV, 276.

76. Ibid., IV, 121-22. For reports by British diplomats, see note 50 above.

77. Ibid., IV, 229-30, 323-36, 238, 240, 242, 244.

78. Ibid., IV, 248, 250-63.

79. Cited in Jacob M. Price, *The Tobacco Adventure to Russia* (Phila-delphia, 1961), vol. 51, Pt. 1 in *Transactions of the American Philosophical Society*, p. 22.

80. For details, see ibid., pp. 23-24. See also Dietrich Gerhard, *England und der Aufstieg Russlands* (Munich-Berlin, 1933), pp. 35-37. Our interpretation provides further data regarding the background of that "opening up" of the old Muscovy Company, the transformation of which into the Russia Company led to an impressive expansion of Anglo-Russian trade after 1699, a date which Gerhard considers as a turning point. For this mutually advantageous strengthening ot commercial ties, stimulated largely by Russia's constant need for credit and by the Royal Navy's growing demand for naval stores, timber and pig iron during a period of empire building and global contest with France, cf. ibid., pp. 38-81 and passim.

81. Historical Manuscript Commission, 58, *Calendar of the Manu-scripts of the Marquis of Bath*, 3 vols. (London, 1904-1908), III, *Prior Papers*, pp. 149-51. The Commissioners of Trade and Plantations to the Lord Justices, Aug. 20, 1697. See also Trumbull to Blathwayt, Aug. 16, Blathwayt to Prior, Aug. 29, Prior to Blathwayt, Sep. 2 and 10, 1697 and Memoir delivered by Matthew Prior to the Secretary of the Russian Am-bassadors, Oct. 24, 1697, ibid., pp. 148, 155, 157, 160 and 181-82, respectively.

82. Ibid., pp. 153-54.

83. Prior to Trumbull, Aug. 23, 1697 and Prior to the Marquis of Winchester, Sept. 13, 1697, ibid., pp. 151-52 and 161, respectively.

84. Prior to Trumbull, Sep. 13, 1697. Ibid., p. 161.

85. Luttrell, *Diary*, IV, 262-76.

86.   Ibid., IV, 278. Similarly revealing is another entry from the end of September: "*our new king* is marching towards Warsaw, where the French party are all in arms. . . . " Ibid., IV, 284. Emphasis added.

87.   Ibid., IV, 286-88, 190-94, 197, 301, 306-308; V, 192, 358, 446; Oscar Halecki, *Borderlands of Western Civilization* (New York, 1952), p. 246.

88.   Luttrell, *Diary*, IV, 286.

89.   A. Lentin, *Voltaire and Catherine the Great.* Selected correspondence. With a Foreword by Elizabeth Hill (Cambridge, 1974), pp. 5-8; Theodore Besterman, *Voltaire*, 3d ed. (Chicago, 1976), p. 362.

90.   Besterman, ed., *Voltaire, Correspondence*, XVIII (1971), 120-21. To Ivan Ivanovich Shuvalov, Aug. 7, 1757. D7336. The letter also contains some information on Voltaire's sources, mentioned in the Historical and Critical Preface: it was sent with the first eight chapters of his book. Cf. Voltaire's exchange with Fedor Pavlovich Veselovsky, Feb. 16 and 19, 1757. Ibid., XVII (1971), 454-55, 461-62. D7160 and D7169.

91.   Besterman, ed., *Voltaire. Correspondence*, I (1968), 359. To Nicolas Claude Thieriot, May 15, 1729(?). D360. Cf. Besterman, *Voltaire*, p. 213, n. 56.

92.   Hill, "Foreword," in Lentin, *Voltaire and Catherine the Great*, pp. 11-28.

93.   Ibid., p. 22. For the improvement of Franco-Russian relations in the wake of the "diplomatic revolution of 1756," and other fine points, see Gaston Zeller, *Les temps modernes, II, De Louis XIV à 1789.* Vol. III in Pierre Renouvin, ed., *Histoire des relations internationales* (Paris, 1955), pp. 227-28, 250-51.

94.   Voltaire, *Siècle de Louis XIV*, 3 vols., *Oeuvres Complètes de Voltaire*, XXII-XXIV (1785), vol. 2 (XXIII), pp. 233-35. Both here, and in his earlier work on Charles XII of Sweden, Voltaire mentioned the negotiations between Radzejowski, the cardinal-primate of Poland and the French ambassador, the Abbé de Polignac, aimed at offering the Polish crown to Conti. "But," according to Voltaire, "money and the troops of Saxony triumphed over these negotiations." Voltaire, *Histoire de Charles XII*, *Oeuvres Complètes de Voltaire* (1785), XXVIII, 108.

95.   Voltaire, *Siècle de Louis XIV*, vol. 2, p. 236.

96.   Voltaire, *Histoire de Russie*, p. 143.

97.   Ibid., p. 144.

98. Besterman, *Voltaire,* pp. 86-87, 625-26. Cf. ibid., pp. 53, n. 33, 301, 658.

99. M. Michaud, ed., *Biographie Universelle, ancienne et moderne,* Nouvelle édition, 45 vols. (Paris 1843-65), IX, 119; Voltaire, *Siècle de Louis XIV,* vol. 1, p. 12 and vol. 2, p. 234.

100. Halecki, *Borderlands,* p. 246.

101. "Lettre de Voltaire à Milord Harvey, Garde des Sceaux d'Angle-terre," 1740, preceding the introduction of the 1768 Geneva edition of the *Siècle de Louis XIV* considered as "definitive" by Voltaire. Reprinted in Voltaire, *Siècle de Louis XIV,* Nouvelle edition annotée par Charles Louandre (Paris, n.d.), pp. vii-viii and xi; Voltaire to Louis César de La Baume Le Blanc, duc de la Vallière, [c. 25 April, 1761], D9754 in Bester-man, ed., *Voltaire, Correspondence,* XXIII, 179. In another letter written about the same time, I. I. Shuvalov informed Voltaire about the sending of additional materials for his "noble work" from St. Petersburg. Apr. 11/12 (O.S.), 1761, Shuvalov to Voltaire, ibid., XXIII, 174.

102. Burnet, *History of His Own Time,* IV, 359-60.

103. Ibid., IV, 360-61. Cf. note 50 above.

104. Halecki, *Borderlands,* p. 224.

105. Voltaire, *Siècle de Louis XIV,* vol. 2, pp. 287-89.

106. Voltaire, *Histoire de Russie,* pp. 7-8.

107. For Voltaire's flattery of Louis XV, see Peter Gay, *The Enlighten-ment* (New York, 1966), p. 281; of the Empresses Elizabeth and Catherine II, Lentin, *Voltaire and Catherine the Great,* passim and above.

108. Voltaire, *Histoire de Charles XII,* pp. 29-31.

109. M. S. Anderson, *Britain's Discovery of Russia* (London, 1958), p. 50.

110. For previous Muscovite diplomatic missions to England and fur-ther references regarding Russo-British relations, see Igor Vinogradoff, "Russian Missions to London, 1569-1687: Seven Accounts By the Masters of the Ceremonies," *Oxford Slavonic Papers* (cited hereafter as *OSP*), New Series, XIV (1981), 36-72 and I. F. Martynov, "Prince P. S. Prozorovsky's Ambassadorial Speech to King Charles II," *OSP,* N.S. XIII (1980), 50-57.

111. Anderson, *Britain's Discovery of Russia,* pp. 50-53; Sir A. W. Ward and G. P. Gooch, eds., *The Cambridge History of British Foreign Policy,* 3 vols. (New York, 1922-23), I, 63-64.

112. See par. 5 of the treaty in *Pis'ma i Bumagi,* II, 176-77.

113. *The Diary of General Patrick Gordon,* pp. 99 and 181. (Entry of March 12, 1667, and Copy of the Factory [Power of Attorney] Sent to John Gordon of Nethermuir, and Patrick Gordon of Cults, January, 1694, respectively.) See also S. Konovalov, "Patrick Gordon's Dispatches from Russia, 1667" and "Sixteen Further Letters of General Patrick Gordon," *OSP,* XI (1964), 8-16 and XIII (1967), 72-95, respectively, and id., "England and Russia: Two Missions, 1666-1668," ibid., XIII, 47-71. In our text on pp. 6-7 above, in Burnet's sermon, cf. ". . . a much greater King . . . a mighty Northern Emperour . . . to . . . enlarge his Empire . . ."

114. Luttrell, *Diary,* IV, 265-66, 273-75, 280 passim.

115. See e.g. Peter to Romodanovskii, Apr. 8 and end of May 1697, *Pis'ma i Bumagi,* I, 145 and 162, respectively.

116. Grönebaum, *Frankreich in Ost- und Nordeuropa,* pp. 124 and 186, n. 6, and Marc Szeftel, "The Title of the Muscovite Monarch up to the End of the Seventeenth Century," *Canadian-American Slavic Studies,* XIII (1979), 72-76 and 79, n. 59. For the first occurrence of the title "Emperor of all Russia" in an official document sent to Ivan IV over the signatures of Queen Mary and her husband King Philip II in 1555, see the Preface in F. de Martens, ed., *Recueil des Traités et Conventions,* conclus par le Russie avec les puissances étrangères. Publié d'ordre du Ministère des Affaires Etrangères. Vol. IX, *Traités avec l'Angleterre. 1710-1801* (St. Petersburg, 1892, Kraus reprint, 1969), p. VIII. For examples of the use of the title "Emperour" in reference to the rulers of Muscovy in sixteenth and seventeenth century English official documents, see Vinogradoff, "Russian Missions," pp. 43, 45-50. But, as pointed out by Vinogradoff, after Lord Carlisle's mission to Moscow in 1663-64, the British took note, despite Russian resentment, "that the 'Czar' should not be called Emperor," although the tsar's wife continued to be referred to as "Empress" in later documents, too. Ibid., pp. 51, 56, 58. Cf. also N. E. Evans, "The Anglo-Russian Royal Marriage Negotiations of 1600-1603," *SEER,* LXI (1983), 363, 368, 373-74, 377-78, 382, 387 and Samuel H. Baron, "Osip Nepea and the Opening of Anglo-Russian Commercial Relations," *OSP,* N.S. XI (1978), 60-62. In the English text, as Professor Stephen N. Baxter noted, the word "empire" may simply mean "sovereign state." But the Utrecht address, in its original form, was not given in English although the English version which we have seems the closest (albeit translated) text of it.

117. For the Hungarian-Transylvanian Prince Francis II Rákóczi's idea

of an *imperium orientale* under Peter I, set forth about a dozen years later (1709), see Béla Köpeczi, *A Rákóczi-szabadságharc és Franciaország* (Rákóczi's Freedom Fight and France; Budapest, 1966), p. 233, n. 74.

118. For the text of the alliance between Muscovy and Brandenburg, see *Pis'ma i Bumagi*, I, 174-78. Cf. also Bogoslovskii, *Petr I*, II, 88-96, 129.

119. Massie, *Peter the Great*, pp. 197-98.

120. See the review by Claes Peterson in *Slavic Review*, XLI (1982), 703. The tsar's promise to grant to William's "industrious subjects . . . greater immunities than ever" in the sphere of trade may have been particularly appealing to the British, who, for over thirty years, indeed since the Stuart Restoration, had tried, in vain, the reestablishment of those commercial privileges which they had enjoyed prior to the execution of Charles I in Muscovy for almost a century. Cf. Konovalov, "England and Russia: Two Missions, 1666-1668," and Vinogradoff, "Russian Missions to London, 1569-1687," as cited in notes 113 and 110, respectively.

121. Hatton, *Charles XII*, p. 102; Wittram, *Peter I*, I, 161.

122. Arcadius Kahan, "Observations on Petrine Foreign Trade," *Canadian-American Slavic Studies*, VIII (1974), 222.

123. Ibid., p. 236; Ragnhild Hatton, *Europe in the Age of Louis XIV* (New York, 1969), pp. 110-111. For the Muscovite tradition of politically motivated decision-making in commercial affairs, cf. Baron, "Osip Nepea and the Opening of Anglo-Russian Commercial Relations," p. 63.

124. Blathwayt's report of Oct. 8, 1697, as cited by Price, *The Tobacco Adventure*, p. 25.

125. Martens, ed., *Traités avec l'Angleterre*, pp. 2-4; Price, *The Tobacco Adventure*, pp. 26-31, 40-47. The Russian text of the agreement was published in *Pis'ma i Bumagi*, I, 243-49. For further reference, cf. Wittram, *Peter I*, I, 159 and 429, n. 75.

126. Baxter, *William III*, p. 363; Robb, *William of Orange*, II, 424.

127. Ian Grey, "Peter the Great in England," *History Today*, VI (1956), 232.

128. Grew, *William Bentinck and William III*, p. 279; Robb, *William of Orange*, II, 498.

129. Luttrell, *Diary*, IV, 274. Cf. note 174 below: "Les deux Princes en Se prirent La main en Signe d'amitié."

130. Luttrell, *Diary*, IV, 290.

131. Luttrell's entry is dated October 12, Carmarthen's letter November

9, 1697, both O.S. For a contemporary Russian translation of the letter, cf. Ustrialov, *Istoriya Petra Velikago*, III, 466-67. For Peter's expression of gratitude for the royal gift, see ibid., III, 89-90.

132. Ibid., III, 466. Emphasis added.

133. Luttrell, *Diary*, IV, 285. For negotiations aimed at transferring to Poland substantial naval and land forces previously fighting the French in the West and of imperial troops in Hungary participating in the anti-Turkish campaigns and at deploying them after the Ryswick treaty against Conti, see Bogoslovskii, *Petr I*, II, 243-45.

134. The text of A / CONGRATULATORY / POEM, / To the High and Mighty / CZAR OF MUSCOVY, / ON HIS ARRIVAL IN ENGLAND / On *Tuesday* the 11th of this Instant *January*, 1697/8. was published in Leo Loewenson, "People Peter the Great met in England. Moses Stringer, Chymist and Physician," *SEER*, XXXVII (1958-59), 459-60. Emphases in original. Cf. A. G. Cross, "'O thou, great monarch of a pow'rful reign!': English Bards and Russian Tsars," *OSP*, N.S., XV (1982), 80-82.

135. See note 33 above.

136. Loewenson, "Some Details of Peter the Great's Stay in England in 1698," pp. 432-42; Luttrell, *Diary*, IV, 258, 290, 296, 301-302, 307, 318.

137. Ibid., IV, 330-31; Loewenson, "Some Details," pp. 434-35, 438; Grey, "Peter the Great in England," pp. 226-28.

138. Luttrell, *Diary*, IV, 340; Loewenson, "Some Details," p. 438.

139. Bogoslovskii, *Petr I*, II, 293-388; Grey, *Peter the Great*, pp. 114-24; Grey, "Peter the Great in England," pp. 229-33.

140. Luttrell, *Diary*, IV, 339.

141. Ustrialov, *Istoriya Petra Velikago*, III, 101; Grey, "Peter the Great in England," p. 234.

142. Ibid., p. 232.

143. Luttrell, *Diary*, IV, 326-27, 349, 352, 357.

144. Cf. the letters of Lord Villiers and the Earl of Jersey to the Duke of Shrewsbury, Sept. 24 and Oct. 18, 1697, respectively, in Cox, *Correspondence*, pp. 374 and 376-77; Spielman, *Leopold I*, pp. 172-73.

145. Grew, *William Bentnick and William III*, pp. 341-43, 351-54; Van der Zee, *William and Mary*, pp. 440-46; Baxter, *William III*, pp. 365-70.

146. Constantin de Grunwald, *Peter the Great* (London, 1956), pp. 88, 114.

147. Ustrialov, *Istoriya Petra Velikago,* III, 107-108; Bogoslovskii, *Petr I,* II, 490; Wittram, *Peter I,* I, 161 and 430, n. 84. For William's exclusion of most of his English ministers including the secretary of state from his secret negotiations with France, see Coxe, *Correspondence,* pp. 371, 381.

148. Bogoslovskii, *Petr I,* II, 380, 412-17.

149. For a copy of the May 31, 1698 Latin letter of Augustus, see the *"Copia plenipotentiae pro me C. Khinsky ad Subscribendam declarationem Turcis in p[unc] to pacis faciendam ad 23 Juny [1698]"* in *Türkei* I, Karton 165, Juni 1698, fol. 82. *Haus-, Hof- und Staatsarchiv* (hereafter *HHStA*), Vienna. Cf. ill. no. 8.

150. Wittram, *Peter I,* I, 161.

151. Schuyler, *Peter the Great,* I, 312-13; Bogoslovskii, *Petr I,* II, 456-66, 474-76.

152. Ibid., II, 467-70; Posselt, *Lefort,* II, 486-87.

153. Ibid., II, 487-94; Bogoslovskii, *Petr I,* II, 477-81. See also Spielman, *Leopold I,* pp. 167-68; McKay, *Prince Eugene,* pp. 52-54; Alfred Arneth, *Prinz Eugen von Savoyen,* 3 vols. (Vienna, 1858), I, 129-30; Braubach, *Prinz Eugen,* I, 178-79. For specific references to the tsar's negotiations with Count Kinsky, the mediation of the Maritime Powers in Istanbul, as well as for the Turkish, Polish, Venetian and Austrian views set forth in preparation for the Congress of Carlowitz, cf. Joseph v. Hammer-Purgstall, *Geschichte des Osmanischen Reiches,* 10 vols. (Graz, 1963), VI, 652-64, passim, in Series A, Joseph v. Hammer-Purgstall, *Werke,* I, ed. Franz Sauer. See also the Venetian ambassador's reports in Joseph Fiedler, ed., *Die Relationen der Botschafter Venedigs über Deutschland und Österreich im siebzehnten Jahrhundert,* in *Fontes Rerum Austriacarum;* Zweite Abtg., Diplomataria et acta, XXVII (Vienna, 1867), 350-65, 427-32 and *Dispacci di Germania,* vol. 39, esp. pp. 150-88. *HHStA,* Vienna. The most detailed documentation reflecting the Moscovite delegation's "presence" in Vienna and fears lest Peter's demands frustrate the negotiations already begun can be found in *Türkei* I (*Turcica*), Kartons 165 and 166 (June-August, 1698). While the British mediator, Ambassador Lord Paget, who was travelling with the camp of the Grand Vizir from Constantinople to Belgrade kept on repeating his warning of June 19, 1698, that *"la porte etant presentement tout disposé a vouloir sincerement la paix"* and pressed Kinsky *"pour prevenir aux accidans qui pourroint arriver a detourner les bonnes dispositions,"* the imperial envoy in Warsaw, Count Sedlnitzky,

reported the same day that *"der TZarr sehr allarmiret gewesen seye"* by Leopold's receipt of the Turkish peace proposals. In order to avoid complications, it was decided at a special conference held on June 30, one week after the emperor nominated Kinsky as his plenipotentiary to make peace with Turkey, that the tsar's audience with Leopold should take place only after the departure of Paget's secretary from Vienna so that the Muscovites would not get an opportunity to set forth new demands, delay the courier, aggravate the mediator and risk the retraction of the Turkish proposals. On July 3, in the midst of discussions with the Russians, Kinsky informed Paget that the King of Poland *"ne s'oppose pas au congrès, mais aussi ne se declaretil pas Sur l'acceptation, où rejet de l'Uti possidetis. Pour ce qu'est du P. Czar de Moscovie maintenant present icy depuis 6 ou 7 jours, nous en traitons avec luy, et J'auray l'honneur d'aviser à V[otre] E[xcellence] du Succès de ce negoce en peu de jours"*. Three weeks later, Paget's letter again cautioned that the *uti possidetis* must apply to Poland and Muscovy as well lest the Turks take advantage of the disunity of the allies. He reiterated again his warning on August 12 in answer to Kinsky's letter of August 2 informing the British ambassador of the tsar's departure from Vienna two days earlier. *Türkei* I, 1698. Karton 165, Juni: pp. 58-63, 78-90, 119-25; Juli: pp. 8-9, 66-82, 125-26; Karton 166, August: pp. 1, 95-96, 107-108. *HHStA,* Vienna. Cf. ill. nos. 7-11. For directing me to the archival materials pertinent to the preparations for the peace negotiations at Carlowitz, I am in the Debt of Drs. Christiane Thomas and Ernst Petritsch, Archivists, in the *Österreichisches Staatsarchiv,* Vienna, Austria.

154. For the Russian inquiry submitted for the emperor's consideration on June 21, the conversation with Kinski on June 26, 1698, as well as the text of the Russian proposals of the same date, see *Pis'ma i Bumagi,* I, 258-63. The German and Latin translations of the three questions raised by the tsar on July 2 and the Austrian replies of July 4 to them as well as the report of July 5 on Peter's reaction to the answers are in *Türkei* I, 1698. Karton 265: Juli: pp. 3-7, 34-35, 50-60. *HHStA,* Vienna. Earlier, in the Autumn of 1697, ironically, the emperor protested in vain against "the desertion of his allies," England, Holland, and Spain, who had signed the Ryswick treaty with France before he did. See Coxe, *Correspondence,* pp. 378-380.

155. A. V. Florovskii, "Russko-Avstriiskie otnosheniia v epokhu Petra Velikogo," *Acta Universitatis Carolinae, Historica,* II (Prague, 1955), 7-10.

156. For an earlier Dutch initiative in Moscow aiming at an anti-Swedish coalition, cf. Jozef Gierowski and Andrzej Kaminski, "The Eclipse of Poland" in Bromley, ed., *The Rise of Great Britain and Russia*, p. 692. For a concise summary, cf. Hatton, *Charles XII,* pp. 102-107. The *Journal de Pierre le Grand depuis l'année 1698 jusqu'à la conclusion de la paix de Neustadt* (Berlin, 1773), pp. 4-5, seems to have preserved the simultaneity of pretexts used by Augustus, who requested Peter's help against "several Poles hostile to" and plotting against him, presumably with Swedish assistance, and Peter, who wished to take revenge for the alleged offense suffered at the hand of the Swedish governor of Riga, Dalberg, at the onset of the Great Embassy's trip.

157. Schuyler, *Peter the Great,* I, 354-56. For the treaties of Carlowitz and Constantinople, see A. N. Kurat and J. S. Bromley, "The Retreat of the Turks, 1683-1730," in Bromley, ed., *The Rise of Great Britain and Russia,* pp. 626-27. For the advantages gained by Russia at Carlowitz, cf. Bogoslovskii, *Petr I,* III, 433-34. For the significance of Carlowitz in the history of the Ottoman Empire, see Stanford Shaw, *History of the Ottoman Empire and Modern Turkey,* 2 vols. (Cambridge, 1976), I, 223-25.

158. The text of the English translation of the Russian original of July 29, 1699 and preserved in London among the *State Papers, Russia*, No. 6, was printed in *Pis'ma i Bumagi,* I, 291-93.

159. Emphasis added.

160. J. S. Bromley, "Introduction" in Bromley, ed., *The Rise of Great Britain and Russia,* p. 2.

161. Hatton, *Charles XII,* pp. 105-107.

162. Bogoslovskii, *Petr I,* III, 441-45.

163. Ragnhild Hatton, "Charles XII and the Great Northern War" and M. S. Anderson, "Russia under Peter the Great and the Changed Relations of East and West," both in Bromley, ed., *The Rise of Great Britain and Russia,* pp. 675-77 and 734-38; Waliszewski, *Peter the Great,* pp. 341-47 and 358-91; André, *Louis XIV et L'Europe,* pp. 322, 352; Walter Kirchner, *Commercial Relations Between Russia and Europe 1400 to 1800* (Bloomington, Ind., 1966), pp. 133-34; L. A. Nikoforov, *Russko-angliiskie otnosheniia pri Petre* (Moscow, 1950), pp. 29-30.

164. The most comprehensive modern treatment of Franco-Hungarian relations in the Age of Louis XIV is Béla Köpeczi's *A Rákóczi-szabadságharc és Franciaország* (cf. n. 117 above). Rákóczi's relations with Peter the

Great are discussed on pp. 163-167, 177-78, 184, 215-18, 266, 326. For further references, see below.

165. Robert Mandrou, *Louis XIV en son temps* (Paris, 1973), pp. 514-16; Mark A. Thomson, "Self-Determination and Collective Security as Factors in English and French Foreign Policy, 1689-1718," in Hatton and Bromley, eds., *William III and Louis XIV*, pp. 279-80; Florovskii, "Russko-Avstriiskie otnosheniia," pp. 17-19; János Váradi-Sternberg, *Századok öröksége* (The Legacy of Centuries) (Budapest-Uzhgorod, 1981), pp. 7-88, passim; Kálmán Benda, ed., *Európa és a Rákóczi-szabadságharc* (Europe and the Freedom Fight of Rákóczi) (Budapest, 1980), especially the contributions by B. Köpeczi, K. Benda, K. O. von Aretin, V. A. Artamonov, V. N. Nikoforov, J. Staszewski, G. Jonasson, Gy. Rázsó and J. Váradi-Sternberg, pp. 13-64, 71-82; József Perényi, "II. Rákóczi Ferenc és I. Péter diplomáciai kapcsolatainak kezdetei" (The Beginnings of the Diplomatic Relations of Francis II. Rákóczi and Peter I), in Endre Kovács, ed., *Magyar-orosz történelmi kapcsolatok* (Hungarian-Russian Historical Connections) (Budapest, 1956), pp. 52-95. For a French report on the tsar's effort to enlist the mediation of Louis XIV in his war with Sweden through the French agent accredited to Rákóczi, see the excerpts translated from the French manuscript *"Relation abbrégée de ce qui est passé dans la guerre d'Hongrie depuis le commencement de la campagne de 1705 jusqu'au mois de mars 1708, par Lemaire ingénieur, ayant service en ce pays"* in Béla Köpeczi and R. Ágnes Várkonyi, eds., *Rákóczi tükör* (Rákóczi Mirror), 2 vols. (Budapest, 1973), II, 251-52. For Rákóczi's negotiations with Moscow, see ibid., II, 268-77; cf. János Pulay's memorandum ibid., II, 412-17 and the diary of Ádám Szathmáry-Király, which describes Peter's personal contact during his trip in Poland with Rákóczi between mid-May and late September, 1711, ibid., II, 419-25. During his visit to France in 1717, the tsar invited the exiled Rákóczi to dinner on one occasion. Ibid., II, 451. For references to and Hungarian translations of documents pertinent to repeated Anglo-Dutch efforts to mediate between the emperor and the Hungarian insurgents between March 1704 and July 1706, see ibid., II, 5-67. For simultaneous, and ambiguous, Russian offers of the Polish crown to Prince Eugene of Savoy, Rákóczi, and the sons of the late Polish king John Sobieski, in the spring of 1707, cf. Grey, *Peter the Great*, pp. 266-67; Wittram, *Peter I*, 284-86.

166. A Hungarian translation of the Latin and Russian original texts

appeared in Sándor Márki, *Nagy Péter czár és II. Rákóczi Ferencz szövet-
sége 1707-ben* (The Alliance of Tsar Peter the Great and Francis II.
Rákóczi in 1707) (Budapest, 1913), pp. 89-93. Cf. *Pis'ma i Bumagi*, vol.
VI, Pt. 2 (St. Petersburg, 1912), pp. 73-80 and ill. no. 12. For mutual suspicions of Rákóczi's and Peter's agents in Constantinople and for the Russian accusations regarding the alleged spying of Rákóczi's resident in Moscow, see Orest Subtelny, "'Peter I's Testament': A Reassessment," *The
Slavic Review*, XXXIII (1974), 664-67. According to the author, Rákóczi
"found it in his interest to develop better relations with Peter I" in 1708.
As indicated above, the improvement of Muscovite-Hungarian relations
began earlier.

   167. For the repudiation of Peter's two attempts (in 1708 and 1710)
to mediate between Rákóczi and Vienna by the latter and the broader context of the effort, cf. János Váradi Sternberg, "Rákóczi diplomáciai be-
szélgetése és levelezése Kurakin herceggel" (Rákóczi's Diplomatic Conversation and Correspondence with Prince Kurakin), in Béla Köpeczi,
Lajos Hopp and Ágnes R. Várkonyi, *Rákóczi tanulmányok* (Rákóczi
Studies, Budapest, 1980), pp. 686-87, 691. For a survey of Anglo-Dutch
mediations, see István Bárczy, "A Rákóczi-szabadságharc angol-holland
diplomáciája" (The Anglo-Dutch Diplomacy during Rákóczi's Freedom
Fight), ibid., pp. 267-87. After Rákóczi's defeat, about one thousand
Hungarian insurgents crossed the Carpathian mountains under the command of a Russian colonel. Of them, 450 men joined the Russian forces
in the campaign of the Pruth against the Turks, while the balance entered the Polish service. V. A. Artamonov, "Magyarország és az orosz-lengyel
szövetség" (Hungary and the Russo-Polish Alliance), in Benda, ed., *Európa
és a Rákóczi szabadságharc,* p. 49. Cf. *Pis'ma i Bumagi*, XI, Pt. 1, pp. 225
and 493 (Doc. 4439 and note), 527-29 (note pertinent to Doc. 4481); XI,
Pt. 2, pp. 40, 46 (Docs. 4623-34), 370, 413 (notes pertinent to Docs. 4616
and 4706). For Austrian protests against Peter's treaty with and support
of Rákóczi as well as a request for his extradition (which was refused)
and further references, see ibid., XI, Pt. 2, pp. 178, 180, 182 (Docs. 4812-
13), 503, 505-506 (notes pertinent to Docs. 4812-13), 583 (note pertinent
to Doc. 4912). For the threat posed by the Rákóczi uprising to the Habsburg Empire and its British ally's view of it in early 1704, cf. the contemporary account of Burnet, first published in 1723: " . . . the emperor was
reduced to the last extremities; the elector of Bavaria was master of the

Danube all down to Passau and the malecontents in Hungary were making a formidable progress. . . . Vienna would be probably besieged on both sides; and it was not in a condition to make a long defense; so the House of Austria seemed lost. Prince Eugene proposed that the Emperor should implore the Queen's protection." Burnet, *History of His Own Time*, V, 143. See also ibid., V, 166-67. Cf. McKay, *Prince Eugene*, pp. 73-74.

168. For the significance of Austrian diplomatic successes "in isolating the northern war from the conflict in the west," cf. Spielman, *Leopold I*, 184.

169. Knoppers, "Tsar Peter I and Utrecht," p. 18. Knopper, of course, did not know the Edinburgh text. Relying on Loewenson, he agrees that "recent discoveries of source material and a more careful analysis of the original sources indicate that Peter did make this speech even though it was probably prepared by someone else beforehand and not as impromptu as first stated." But Knopper also believes that in their two-hour long "private conversation" the monarchs were "assisted only by Nicolass Witsen and Lefort," an assumption implying that the latter served as interpreter and that the earliest text of the speech was committed to paper in French. My interpretation suggests the possibility of the simultaneity or even primacy of the English version(s).

170. For this information, I am in the debt of Dr. Theo Thomassen, Archivist of the First Section in the Algemeen Rijksarchief, Gravenhage, The Netherlands, Letter to author, April 29, 1983.

171. Luttrell, *Diary*, IV, 274.

172. Ibid., IV, 291.

173. Baxter, *William III*, pp. 327, 348-52. My efforts to find some reference to the Utrecht meeting in the Albemarle correspondence in the Public Record Office in London or the Historical Commission have remained fruitless so far.

174. "Mémoires concernant l'histoire et la vie du general et amiral Lefort," Bibliothèque Publique et Universitaire de Genève, Département des manuscrits, Cote Ms. F. 1013, p. 63. I am in the debt of Mr. Thierry Ulmann, Geneva, Switzerland, for providing me with information regarding the manuscript the existence of which was unknown to me and also for kindly sending me a xerox copy of the passage concerning the *Entrevue du Czar & du Roy Guillaum a Utrecht*. Referring to the Muscovite ambassadors' arriving in Holland, the pertinent paragraph reads:

Avant que de prendre audience des Estats Generaux ils allerent a Utrech avec Le Czaar environ Le 10e du 7bre où ils se rendirent Le matin. Sa Maj^{té} Britannique S'y rendit trois heures apres & descendit a L'auberge ou Le Czaar estoit Logé. Les Ambassadeurs Moscovites allerent dés aussitost complimenter Le Roy Guillaume dans Sa Chambre. Le General Le Fort qui portoit La parole apres quelques entretiens proposa a S.M.B. Si Elle n'auroit pas pour agreable de voir Le Czaar qui estoit dans La Chambre prochaine. Le Roy L'ayant agrée y passa avec huit personnes. Les deux Princes en Se Saluant Se prirent La main en Signe d'amitié. Leur conversation roula sur Les affaires de Pologne, & sur La paix qui Se traitoit a Ruiswik; apres S'estre donné des marques reciproques d'affection Le Czaar offrit du vin au Roy, Lequel le remercia. Le Roy a Son tour invita Le Czaar a disner, mais quoy qu'il L'eut comme accepté il S'en excusa Sur Le Champ disant qu'il Seroit veu de trop de monde; Le Roy Se dit tres Satisfait & fort joyeux de cette conference qui fust assès Longue & dont Le General Le Fort fust Seul L'interprete: Le Roy trouva Le Czaar bien fait & d'un raisonnem^t. Solide. See also ill. no. 6 and Lowenson, "The First Interviews," pp. 313-14 and n. 74 above.

175. The *Calendar of State Papers, Domestic,* which includes summaries of the collection of semi-private papers known as King William's Chest, does not seem to contain any reference to the tsar's speech at Utrecht which is not mentioned by British representatives in Holland either. I am in the debt of Dr. Norman Evans, head of the Search Department of the Public Record Office, London, Chancery Lane, for having kindly checked the *Calendar* and the reports from British representatives in the *State Papers,* Holland, SP 84/222 and Russia, SP 91 in response to my inquiry. Letter to the author, February 18, 1983.

176. P. W. J. Riley, *King William and the Scottish Politicians* (Edinburgh, 1979), pp. 29 and 44, n. 50. In the index, on p. 913, George Gordon is erroneously identified as the fifteenth earl of Sutherland. Cf. Sir William Fraser, *The Sutherland Book,* 3 vols. (Edinburgh, 1892), I, 294-303, III, 216.

177. Ibid., I, 315-22, II, 18-23, 197-99.

178. "Chairman's Afterword" in A. G. Cross, ed., *Great Britain and Russia in the Eighteenth Century: Contacts and Comparisons* (Newtonville, Mass., 1979), p. 321.

179. Grey, *Peter the Great,* pp. 140-46, 168-69; Ustrialov, *Istoriya Petra Velikago,* III, 201-45, 368-72; Bogoslovskii, *Petr I,* III, 26-126, IV, 405-23. Cf. the penetrating analysis of the war with Sweden in Wittram, *Peter I,* I, 196-232.

180. Lemaire, *"Relation abbrégée de ce qui s'est passé dans la guerre d'Hongrie,"* in Köpeczi and Várkonyi, eds., *Rákóczi tükör,* II, 224, 286; "Beniczky Gáspár naplója" (The Diary of Gáspár Beniczky, excerpts), ibid., II, 369; János Pulay, "A szatmári békesség" (Memoir on the Peace of Szatmár, excerpts), ibid., II, 412, and ibid., II, 560 (editors' annotation). Regarding the elector of Bavaria, see in addition to the references in note 35 above, Max Braubach, "Die Politik des Kurfürsten Max Emanuel von Bayern im Jahre 1702," in id., *Diplomatie und geistiges Leben im 17. und 18. Jahrhundert* (Bonn, 1969), pp. 148-84.

181. Thomas Babington Macauley, *History of England from the Accession of James the Second,* 5 vols. (New York, n.d.), V, 310-11, cited also in Leo Loewenson, "Some Details of Peter the Great's Stay in England in 1698: Neglected British Material," *SEER,* XL (1962), 431; Wittram, *Peter I,* I, 157. For further references to the literature, cf. ibid., I, 429, n. 72.

182. Cox, *Correspondence,* pp. 509, 513-16, 519, 547-48, 552, 565-67, 571-77.

183. Burnet, *A Sermon Preached before the King at Whitehall,* pp. 23-28.

184. Ibid., p. 13.

185. Cracraft, *The Church Reform of Peter the Great,* pp. 32-37. For the broader aspects of the problem, cf. Donald W. Treadgold, *The West in Russia and China,* 2 vols. (Cambridge, 1973), I, 86-89.

186. Claes Peterson, *Peter the Great's Administrative and Judicial Reforms* (Stockholm, 1979), pp. 411-17 and passim.

187. Wittram, *Peter I,* I, 160; id., *Russia and Europe* (London, 1973), pp. 48-50; Max J. Okenfuss, "Russian Students in Europe in the Age of Peter the Great," in J. G. Garrard, ed., *The Eighteenth Century in Russia* (Oxford, 1973), p. 142.

188. A. G. Cross, "'By the Banks of the Thames': Russians in Eighteenth-Century Britain" and A. S. Fedorov, "Russia and Britain in the Eighteenth Century: A Survey of Economic and Scientific Links," both in Cross, ed., *Great Britain and Russia in the Eighteenth Century,* pp. 34-35 and 141-42, respectively.

189. Fedorov, "Russia and Britain," ibid., p. 142. For the growing mutual dependence of England and Russia in foreign trade in the last third of the eighteenth century, see Arcadius Kahan, "Eighteenth-Century Russian-British Trade: Russia's Contribution to the Industrial Revolution in Great Britain," ibid., pp. 181-89.

190. Fedorov, "Russia and Britain," ibid., p. 143; G. L. 'E Turner, "Forms of Patronage and Institutionalisation of Science in the Eighteenth Century," Iu. Kh. Kopelevich, "The Creation of the Petersburg Academy of Sciences as a New Type of Scientific and State Institution," both ibid., pp. 198-99 and 205-206, respectively. See also, V. Boss, *Newton and Russia*, pp. 9, 14-20, 40-45, 78-90, 93-96, 103-104 and passim; Alexander Vucinich, *Science in Russian Culture*, 2 vols. (Stanford, Calif., 1963-70), I, 44-45, 49, 65-74.

191. Ibid., I, 60. On the strength of the foregoing, one is tempted to question the suggestion that the date of the beginning of modern Anglo-Russian relations should be fixed for the year 1714, the year of the Elector George of Hanover's accession to the English throne. Cf. K. W. B. Middleton, *Britain and Russia* (London, n.d.), p. 18.

192. Burnet, *History of His Own Time*, IV, 409. Emphasis added.

193. Karl Marx, *Secret Diplomatic History of the Eighteenth Century and the Story of the Life of Lord Palmerston*, ed. Lester Hutchinson (New York, 1969), pp. 63, 85-86, 92-94 and passim.

194. Nikiforov, *Russko-angliiskie otnosheniia pri Petre*, p. 17 (translation mine). The Soviet author, who repeatedly cites Marx's *Secret Diplomatic History* in the Introduction of his work, accuses William III of protecting Sweden against Russia with his efforts at mediating between the two countries in 1700 rather than betraying that country as Marx had claimed. Ibid., 24-25.

195. Ibid., p. 12. For Russian efforts to open trade routes across the Baltic Sea, cf. Walther Kirchner, *The Rise of the Baltic Question* (Newark, Del., 1954), pp. 1-3, 86-122, 254-57.

196. N. E. Evans, "The Anglo-Russian Royal Marriage Negotiations of 1600-1603," *SEER*, LXI (1983), 369. Cf. Vinogradoff, "Russian Missions," p. 40.

197. Ibid., pp. 50-72; Martynov, "Prince P. S. Prozorovsky's Ambassadorial Speech," pp. 50-51.

198. Gerhard, *England und der Aufstieg Russlands*, pp. 8-16, 37-42

and 403; Sir Richard Lodge, "The First Anglo-Russian Treaty," *The English Historical Review*, XLIII (1928), 354-55, 358-60, 373-74. For the French and Russian texts of the treaties of 1734 and 1741 and 1742, cf. Martens, ed., *Traités avec l'Angleterre*, pp. 62-133.

199. Bogoslovskii, *Petr I*, II, 380-412, 490-91; Grey, *Peter the Great*, pp. 123 and 459, n. 32.

200. P. P. Shafirov, *A Discourse Concerning the Just Causes of the War Between Sweden and Russia: 1700-1721*. With an Introduction by William E. Butler (Dobbs Ferry, N.Y., 1973), p. 284. Emphases in the original.

201. For the significance of Shafirov's work, the first original study on international law in the Russian language, see William E. Butler's introduction, ibid., pp. 1-39 and the same author's "Anglo-Russian Diplomacy and the Law of Nations," in Cross, ed., *Great Britain and Russia in the Eighteenth Century*, p. 297. Cf. James Cracraft's review, for some caveats, in *Slavic Review*, XXXIV (1975), 385-86.

202. For the relief brought by the peace of Carlowitz for the Anglo-Dutch alliance in its struggle with France, cf. Baxter, *William III*, p. 369.

203. See note 157 above and the pertinent text. For British and Dutch mediation in Muscovy's disputes with Sweden, going back to the times of James I, cf. Shafirov, *A Discourse*, pp. 265-66, 268-69, 291, 294, 312-13, 316, 330. For Lord Paget's role as the mediator at Carlowitz, see Grey, *Peter the Great*, p. 153.

204. Ibid., pp. 186, 267-71.

205. Ibid., p. 269. See also notes 165-167 above and the relevant text.

206. Ustrialov, *Istoriya Petra Velikago*, III, 487-88 (Append. VII, no. 17).

Champ.
October 1989

STUDIES IN IRISH MANUSCRIPTS / TAIGHDE AR LÁMHSCRÍBHINNÍ

General editor / Eagarthóir ginearálta: Pádraig de Brún

CATALOGUE OF IRISH MANUSCRIPTS

IN THE

UNIVERSITY OF WISCONSIN—MADISON